FROM TECHNICAL SPECIALIST TO SUPERVISOR

Donald Shandler, Ph.D.

A FIFTY-MINUTE™ SERIES BOOK

FROM TECHNICAL SPECIALIST TO SUPERVISOR

Donald Shandler, Ph.D.

CREDITS
Editor: **Sara Schneider**
Typesetting: **ExecuStaff**
Cover Design: **Carol Harris**
Artwork: **Ralph Mapson**

© 1993 by Crisp Publications, Inc.
Printed in the United States of America by Von Hoffmann Graphics, Inc.

CrispLearning.com

00 01 02 03   10 9 8 7 6 5 4 3

Library of Congress Catalog Card Number 92-73846
Shandler, Donald
From Technical Specialist to Supervisor
ISBN 1-56052-194-5

This book is printed on recyclable paper with soy ink.

LEARNING OBJECTIVES FOR:

FROM TECHNICAL SPECIALIST TO SUPERVISOR

The objectives for *From Technical Specialist to Supervisor* are listed below. They have been developed to guide you, the reader, to the core issues covered in this book.

Objectives

- ❑ **1) To recognize the skills needed by technical supervisors**

- ❑ **2) To discuss management styles**

- ❑ **3) To explain communication, motivation, and delegation skills**

Assessing Your Progress

In addition to the learning objectives, Crisp Learning has developed an **assessment** that covers the fundamental information presented in this book. A twenty-five item, multiple choice/true-false questionnaire allows the reader to evaluate his or her comprehension of the subject matter. An answer sheet with a chart matching the questions to the listed objectives is also available. To learn how to obtain a copy of this assessment, please call **1-800-442-7477** and ask to speak with a Customer Service Representative.

Assessments should not be used in any selection process.

PREFACE

An ideal human resource development model provides *technical professionals* with the skills necessary for success as a *technical supervisor* **before** they really need them. But research indicates that this is more the exception than the rule. Since this is true, the following three audiences will benefit from reading and using this book.

1. **Technical experts planning a transition to technical supervision.** It is best to learn what to do before you actually have to do it.

2. **New technical supervisors.** On-the-job training can be quite successful. Read this book within three months of becoming a technical supervisor.

3. **Experienced technical supervisors who have never received any formal training.** Surprisingly, there are many technical supervisors who may have received "field promotions" —a bench scientist on Friday and a technical supervisor on Monday—who have not received any formal supervisory training. It is not too late to step back and learn "how to work smarter—not harder."

Donald Shandler

Donald Shandler

ABOUT THE AUTHOR

Donald Shandler, Ph.D., is founder and president of Organizational Development & Research Associates, Inc., in Columbia, Maryland. OD&R is a comprehensive training and consulting firm specializing in the *assessment*, *selection* and *development* of *managers* and *leaders*.

In addition, Don offers clients extensive experience in addressing the unique developmental needs of professionals, supervisors and managers in technical environments. The American Society of Training and Development, Metropolitan Washington, D.C., chapter, has twice recognized him for efforts in Managing in Technology.

He has presented seminars for technical supervisors and managers for CSX Technology, GTE, The MITRE Corporation, Planning Research Corporation, the Social Security Administration and the Defense Information Systems Agency.

Dr. Shandler holds a Ph.D. from Ohio State University and is an experienced facilitator. He has presented seminars, university courses, papers and lectures throughout the United States and Europe. He welcomes the opportunity to remain in touch with clients, students and readers and can be reached by contacting:

Donald Shandler, Ph.D.
Organizational Development & Research Associates, Inc.
10480 Little Patuxent Parkway, Suite 400
Columbia, Maryland 21044
Phone 410/750-2400
Fax 410/750-3937

Dedication

To my mother and father who have instilled a lifelong love of learning. To my wife, son and daughter who have encouraged me to do what I do best.

And to all the technical professionals, supervisors, managers and leaders who have taught me as much as I, hopefully, have taught them. Special thanks to clients and colleagues who have supported all of the issues that this book addresses.

CONTENTS

CONTENTS (continued)

INTRODUCTION: WHY TECHNICAL SUPERVISING IS UNIQUE

A growing nationwide training and development trend is under way. Organizations are recognizing that *managing in technology* is a unique and challenging experience for the new technical supervisor. The person who moves from the role of technical expert to supervisor learns this quickly. New technical supervisors, more often than not, discover that:

1. **Technical knowledge does not convert to "people" skills.**

   Technologists (scientists, engineers and related professionals) develop sophisticated analytical and reasoning skills as a result of years of technical education. As new technical supervisors, they quickly discover that, while their education places them on top of the technical realm, they now need a new set of interaction skills to deal with people.

2. **"Nontechnical" is no longer "nonintelligent."**

   Technical education (such as for science, engineering, medicine and law) provides precise, perfect solutions to complex problems. Some technical experts have developed the unfortunate bias that "if it can't be measured, it isn't really worthwhile." To some, "nontechnical" means "nonintelligent." They ask, "Why can't people be more like programs?" This mind-set must change quickly for technical experts to be good managers.

3. **"Letting go" early is necessary.**

   Yes, you can do it faster and better than most—perhaps all—of your staff, and it is more gratifying to do it yourself. Your new role as a technical supervisor, however, requires you to gain satisfaction now in helping others do the technical work for you. You must undergo a "power conversion"—that is, convert your technical expertise (one form of power) to people skills (another form of power).

INTRODUCTION (continued)

4. **Managing technical experts can be challenging.**

   "Technical experts," "knowledge workers," the "new professionals" are individuals, like you, who often possess double or triple degrees. Their unique technical expertise is mirrored by their equally focused values, attitudes and personal styles. Each expert has a personal "performance equation." Your job is to find it and manage it.

5. **Your technology framework quickly expands.**

   The move from technical expert to technical supervisor is too often a "trial by error" experience. As a technical expert you often worked alone, or perhaps on a small team, reaching systematic closure to a long-term project. Suddenly your role is expanded. You are now managing concurrent projects and reconciling the often conflicting demands of *people, technology and organizations*. The logical has become chaotic. You need a new set of skills.

6. **Technical supervisors must become organizational realists.**

   As a technical expert, you probably expected your manager to serve as a critical buffer, protecting you from the organizational politics and policies that prevented you from doing your job. Now, as a technical supervisor, you must not only look over your shoulder to take care of those technical professionals just like you, but also spend more time on political issues. "Who are the decision makers I must effectively deal with?" "Where are the champions who will provide support for additional resources for my department?" "How do I sell my ideas in competitive environments?"

This book will address other issues as well. In the meantime, here is the bottom line. While "technical excellence" and "quality assurance" remain critical to your success as a technical supervisor, *people skills, supervisory competencies* and *political realities* are even more important.

P A R T

I

The Transition: Getting Off to a Good Start

MAKE THE TRANSITION A MANAGEABLE PROCESS

The *technical expert* who receives a sudden "field promotion" on Friday and becomes a *technical supervisor* on Monday is often psychologically immobilized. This can be avoided.

- A successful transition from technical expert to supervisor can be accomplished through planning.

- This book will give the reader an opportunity to master the competencies of technical supervision—a combination of knowledge, skill and attitude.

- The new technical supervisor will be given many opportunities to demonstrate his or her abilities. Cumulative personal successes will outperform any momentary setbacks or difficulties.

The Five-Step Transition Process

1. **Prepare to make the transition.**

2. **Master basic interpersonal communication skills.**

3. **Develop an understanding of how to motivate technical experts.**

4. **Learn to delegate effectively to technical professionals.**

5. **Apply the right skills to each situation.**

Note: Remember that each new technical supervisory experience requires new and sharper skills. Your development should be ongoing and manageable. Success will not come by accident.

BEFORE YOU BEGIN THE TRANSITION

Organizations tend to identify high-performing *technical experts* and promote them into *technical supervisors*. This involves two falsely made assumptions. First, technical expertise does not convert into supervisory success. Second, the *competence* (understanding of subject) and *motivation* (desire to perform) that an expert may have for technology may not transfer to competence and motivation for supervision.

Here are four critical questions for the technical expert to address before accepting a position as supervisor:

▶ **Why do I want to become a technical supervisor?**

A wide variety of reasons propels people to become technical supervisors. It is important to identify and reconcile your choice before you start the transition. Failure to do so will inhibit your commitment to supervision.

▶ **Am I prepared to take the risk?**

In this decade of intense change—technological, organizational, economical and global—moving from the role of technical expert to technical supervisor is risky.

More and more double-degreed technical professionals are choosing to maintain a *nonmanagement career path* because, in the 12–18 months they need to establish a firm basis as a technical supervisor, they might lose their cutting-edge technological expertise.

▶ **Am I willing to let go?**

Becoming an effective technical supervisor requires relinquishing old sets of behaviors and assuming new—and often very different—behaviors. Your career as a technical supervisor, and later as a manager, will require you to shift your preferences and skills in many areas.

▶ **Have I identified my supervisory strengths and weaknesses?**

There is no magic formula for successful transitioning from technical expert to supervisor. There is, though, a critically important ''declaration of intent.'' You have to be willing to honestly assess your current supervisory strengths and weakness and ''believe in yourself.''

Now lets close in the lens and give you a chance to examine each of these issues in greater depth.

1. Why Do I Want to Become a Technical Supervisor?

Review your reasons for becoming a technical supervisor and share with others the lessons that you learned from the experience.

Exercise: Select one or more of the following reasons for becoming a technical supervisor and explain the lesson you learned—or might learn—from the experience.

- *I had no choice.* Management placed me in my new role with little discussion and no training.

    Lesson learned: _____

    _____

- *I was chosen to move into supervision and had the opportunity to negotiate on specifics:* when, how, where and the training needed.

    Lesson learned: _____

    _____

WHY DO I WANT TO BECOME A TECHNICAL SUPERVISOR (continued)

- *I initiated the transition for one or more of the following reasons:*

  ☐ a. To make more money

  ☐ b. To gain prestige and status

  ☐ c. To exercise more authority

  ☐ d. To increase my sphere of influence

  ☐ e. To do broader and more interesting work (technical work can become dull)

  ☐ f. To have more opportunities for achievement, recognition, leadership and risk-taking

  ☐ g. Other

    Lessons learned: _____

    _____

From your professional perspective as a technical supervisor, what recommendations would you make to others becoming technical supervisors?

_____

_____

_____

_____

_____

_____

2. Am I Prepared to Take the Risk?

Any career move is risky. The technical expert who chooses to become a technical supervisor may very well have to relinquish the time he or she used before to maintain a high level of technical expertise to time now required for successful supervision.

Exercise: You can minimize your risk-taking by objectively answering these questions. Perhaps you may want to share your responses with a colleague who can provide feedback and guidance.

- **What are my "real" motives for becoming a technical supervisor?**

  If it is the only way to advance in your organization and to increase your income, your ultimate satisfaction and effectiveness may suffer.

  Response: _____

  _____

- **Am I managing a well-planned "career" or just changing "jobs"?**

  Both the individual and the organization have a responsibility to initiate and sustain a realistic, career-path contract. Has this taken place?

  Response: _____

  _____

- **What are my real strengths—technical specialty, supervision or perhaps both?**

  Do you have any previous indicators (such as temporary project management) that you can succeed in this new role?

  Response: _____

  _____

3. Am I Willing to Let Go?

Each of us has preferences for a kind of work and how to do it. But as you move from the role of technical expert to technical supervisor, you need to *let go* of what you *most like to do,* to assume the responsibilities *your new role requires.*

Exercise: Circle the number that most accurately reflects *where you are now.*

As a technical expert I received satisfaction from:

As a technical manager I now emphasize:

1. Technical performance (cost secondary)

   Forecasting, analyzing, controlling costs

1	2	3	4	5	6	7	8	9	10

2. Seeking relationships among technical facts and technological issues

   Seeking relationships among business issues with business leaders

1	2	3	4	5	6	7	8	9	10

3. Evaluating data systems and methods

   Evaluating people's performance

1	2	3	4	5	6	7	8	9	10

4. Seeking additional data

   Making decisions often from insufficient data

1	2	3	4	5	6	7	8	9	10

5. High analytical and technical skills

   High verbal and social skills

1	2	3	4	5	6	7	8	9	10

6. Logic outranking conformity

Responsibility for transmitting and enforcing policy

1   2   3   4   5   6   7   8   9   10

7. Being consulted by people for technical expertise

Spending increasingly more time on counseling, guiding and directing people (who often have greater technical expertise)

1   2   3   4   5   6   7   8   9   10

8. Emphasis on the intuitive and the creative

Being increasingly more sensitive to the feelings, attitudes and beliefs of others

1   2   3   4   5   6   7   8   9   10

9. Striving for the technical idea

Recognizing and accepting organizational hierarchy

1   2   3   4   5   6   7   8   9   10

10. Placing little emphasis on organizational procedures, policies and politics

Placing considerable emphasis on organizational politics and economic realities

1   2   3   4   5   6   7   8   9   10

Summary: Now that you have completed this short "preference assessment," it is time to step back and evaluate where you are and where you need to go. Here are some guidelines.

• If you scored 1–3, you are *reluctant* to let go. These areas need attention.

• If you scored 4–6, you are in *transition*. Keep moving.

• If you scored 7–10, you have *arrived*. Congratulations.

Based on material appearing in J. L. Balderston, "Do You Really Want to Be a Manager?" *Journal of the Society of Research Administration*, IX (Spring 1978): 4.

From Technical Specialist to Supervisor

4. Have I Identified My Supervisory Strengths and Weaknesses?

Supervisory development is a manageable and accessible process. To determine the gaps where you need further training and development, you need to evaluate both your *proficiency* in (how well you can do something) and the *relevance* of (how important a skill is to your job) each of the following nine supervisory functions.

Exercise: Assign two ratings for each of the following supervisory functions. On a scale of 1–5, 5 is the highest and 1 is the lowest. Your developmental needs are greatest where you rank high in relevance and low in proficiency.

Relevance	Proficiency	Functions
5 4 3 2 1	5 4 3 2 1	**Plan.** To decide on the "mission"; to establish strategies for accomplishing the objectives and goals.
5 4 3 2 1	5 4 3 2 1	**Organize.** To establish an organizational structure; to write job descriptions; to decide on the qualifications of people to fit the jobs; to select the right people for the jobs.
5 4 3 2 1	5 4 3 2 1	**Communicate.** To clarify what you expect of each person on the job; to keep people informed; to give instructions and orders so that subordinates understand.
5 4 3 2 1	5 4 3 2 1	**Train and Develop.** To teach subordinates the knowledge, skills and attitudes they need to do their jobs.
5 4 3 2 1	5 4 3 2 1	**Motivate.** To create a climate that encourages subordinates to try to do their best.

5 4 3 2 1   5 4 3 2 1   **Delegate.** To turn over to subordinates part of the manager's job in order to save time; to motivate subordinates by enriching their jobs; to train subordinates; to test subordinates to see how well they can handle new job assignments.

5 4 3 2 1   5 4 3 2 1   **Coach.** To work with subordinates on a continuous basis to help them improve their performance as individuals and as members of a team.

5 4 3 2 1   5 4 3 2 1   **Innovate.** To recommend or initiate changes in the department that will help improve efficiency and morale.

5 4 3 2 1   5 4 3 2 1   **Control.** To establish standards or objectives; to evaluate the performance of each employee against those standards or objectives; to take corrective action if performance is below standard; and to reward and provide positive reinforcement for performance that meets or exceeds the standards.

Summary: Now total the gap between relevance and proficiency (the gap is the total spaces between numbers). Those functions with the largest number need your attention.

_____ Plan   _____ Train and Develop   _____ Coach

_____ Organize   _____ Motivate   _____ Innovate

_____ Communicate   _____ Delegate   _____ Control

Adapted with permission of the publisher, from "Management Development," by Donald L. Kirkpatrick in *Human Resources Management and Development Handbook*, Ed. William R. Tracey, copyright 1985, AMACOM, a division of the American Management Association. All rights reserved.

STARTING THE TRANSITION PROCESS

A change of title and office does not make the technical expert a good technical supervisor. If you can now answer these questions we discussed earlier, you are ready to start the transition process. Place a check mark by each statement for the answer that you believe reflects your current position.

	Yes	No	Maybe
1. I clearly know why I want to become an effective technical supervisor.	☐	☐	☐
2. I am prepared to take the risk.	☐	☐	☐
3. I am willing to let go.	☐	☐	☐
4. I know what my supervisory strengths and weaknesses are.	☐	☐	☐

TIPS FOR MAKING A SMOOTH TRANSITION

Making an Effective Transition

A great deal has been written over the past few years about making the transition into technical supervision and management. Here are recommendations for adjusting smoothly to the change.

► **Find a Coach or Mentor.**

One of the best ways to develop your competencies (knowledge, skills and attitudes) as a technical manager is by finding a coach or mentor who will take you under his or her wing and help you develop.

► **Avoid Predictable Trouble Pockets As You Move into Technical Supervision.**

Research has shown that a series of recurring problems face technical experts who become technical supervisors. Learn from the mistakes of others.

► **Identify and Modify Your Personal Style.**

Understanding yourself and your personal style is critical as you make the transition from technical expert to technical supervisor. In simple terms, by gaining an understanding of your ''self,'' you improve your ability to relate and respond to other people.

In the next section we will give you an opportunity to identify your very own behavioral pattern, the distinct way you think and act.

► **Learn to Understand Other Technical Types.**

Along with learning to understand yourself and the personal styles of others, it is helpful to learn about other ''technical types.'' The very same positive attributes that enable an individual to climb the corporate technical ladder rapidly can inhibit effective performance as a technical supervisor or manager.

STARTING THE TRANSITION PROCESS (continued)

▶ **Maximize Your Assets By Converting Your Technical Power to Personal Power.**

As a technical expert moving into technical supervision, you have a critically important dilemma to reconcile: Rather quickly you need to develop *new nontechnical* powers before your technical expertise slips away.

Much of your effectiveness as a technical supervisor will come from newly acquired personal power. You will need to understand your personality characteristics; identify the characteristics of your subordinates, peers and managers; and understand how the two relate.

▶ **Balance Your Task-Oriented Style with People-Oriented Needs.**

As a technical expert you are educationally conditioned to convert almost any task into a technical task. Such a *task-oriented style* tends to overlook the critical importance of the *people-oriented style.* Your situational leadership skills should help you determine when the task should rightfully be placed ahead of the people. And at other times you will clearly put people ahead of the task. At all times you should consciously try to balance the people and the task.

▶ **Model the Behaviors You Encourage in Others.**

This is a decade of profound change in organizational and human resource management. "Total quality management," "empowerment" and "managing for commitment" all require the new technical supervisor to model the very behaviors needed to build high-performing technical teams. The positive attitude you convey to others and the way you communicate, motivate and delegate can not only fully harness and use your collective resources, but also provide you with an opportunity to showcase your *technical supervisory skills* by modeling *effective supervisor behaviors.* We will learn more about this later.

▶ **Learn the Ballgame and Playing Field—It Is Changing Fast.**

As a technical expert, your work and performance expectations were tightly focused. Technical organizations often develop mini-technical cultures that, while fostering technical excellence, often prevent the individual from observing the big picture.

As a technical supervisor, you should pull back the lens. Your previous world of technical order—often sequential, time-limited projects—has now become a world of concurrent, nonending tasks. It would be very much to your advantage to develop a proactive view of supervising in technology-driven environments.

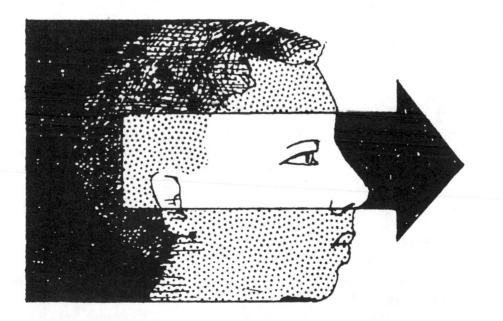

AVOIDING PREDICTABLE TROUBLE POCKETS

More than ten years ago, Michael Badawy wrote in his excellent book, *Developing Managerial Skills in Engineers and Scientists*, about the often "troublesome transition" of technical expert to supervisor. Unfortunately, many of us continue to fail to learn from the past mistakes of others.

New technical supervisors face a series of recurring problems. Which one or two of the following six problem areas are most relevant to your transition?

☐ **Bias Toward Objective Measurement**

Having been trained in the "hard" sciences, technical experts are often more comfortable working with things that they can objectively control and measure. Managers, on the other hand, must rely on intuition and judgment in dealing with attitudes, biases, perceptions, emotions and feelings.

☐ **Paralysis by Analysis**

Technical experts suffer from this "disease": the tendency to wait for all information to be in before they make a decision. In management, you never have all the facts, nor will there ever be a riskless decision.

☐ **Fear of Losing Intimate Contact with Their Fields**

Technologists find it difficult to understand that as managers they must get things done through other people. In their zeal to stay professionally competent, they fail to delegate and tend to handle the technical details themselves.

☐ **Technologists as Introverts**

Research shows that many technical experts tend to be "introverts" rather than "extroverts." Furthermore, this introversion is usually associated with creativity. However, managing a team is an extroverted activity. The "long wolf" nature of many technologists could, therefore, make it doubly difficult for them to function effectively as technical managers.

☐ **Poor Delegators**

Technologists are doers rather than delegators because they believe, rightly or wrongly, that they can perform a task better than anyone else on their staff. Yet, one of the most valuable skills a manager can possess is the ability to delegate.

☐ **Inadequate Interpersonal Skills**

A major source of headaches for managers is "people" problems. Poor interpersonal skills are a major factor in failure among technical managers.

☐ **What transition trouble spots have you experienced?**

_____

_____

Based on material appearing in M. K. Badawy, *Developing Managerial Skills in Engineers and Scientists*, pp. 48–49, 1982. With permission of the publisher, Van Nostrand Reinhold, N.Y.

UNDERSTANDING THE TECHNICAL TYPES

Authors Brian L. Davis and Lila N. Lewey make an interesting observation in their article ''When Techies Manage.'' The very same positive attributes that enable an individual to climb the corporate technical ladder rapidly can inhibit effective performance as a technical supervisor or manager.

From their work with managers who have made the transition from technical expert to manager, they have identified four personality profiles. Each type could improve its effectiveness by modifying its behavior.

Review each of the four predominant technical management types. **Are there any similarities between their behavior and yours?** On the basis of the preferred way of behaving, what recommendations would you make to improve managerial effectiveness? Place a check mark in each box that might apply to you. When you are done, compare your answers with the authors' on pages 21–22.

Thinkers, Gurus, Track Stars and Vulcans

Technical Management Type

Ways to Improve Managerial Effectiveness

The Thinker

☐ Suffers from an overdeveloped set of analytical skills

_____

_____

☐ Has always placed a premium on critical thinking ability

_____

_____

☐ Believes that if given enough time, he or she can arrive at a perfect solution

_____

_____

☐ Suffers from ''paralysis by analysis''

_____

_____

Technical Guru

☐ The only source of power this person respects is technical expertise

_____

_____

☐ Disdains anything that resembles organizational policy

_____

_____

☐ Manages others in the manner he or she likes to be managed (left alone)

_____

_____

☐ Refuses to build networks and keeps things "strictly business"

_____

_____

Track Star

☐ By far the most competitive

_____

_____

☐ Rises on individual efforts and has a tremendous achievement orientation

_____

_____

☐ Demonstrates pride and a keen sense of project ownership

_____

_____

☐ Is highly critical if personal standards are not met

_____

_____

UNDERSTANDING THE TECHNICAL TYPES (continued)

The Vulcan

☐ Logic is the Vulcan's creed

_____
_____

☐ If it isn't totally logical, it doesn't make sense

_____
_____

☐ Tends to be void of emotion and believes feelings have no place in decision making

_____
_____

☐ Tends to set arbitrary policy without consulting those directly involved

_____
_____

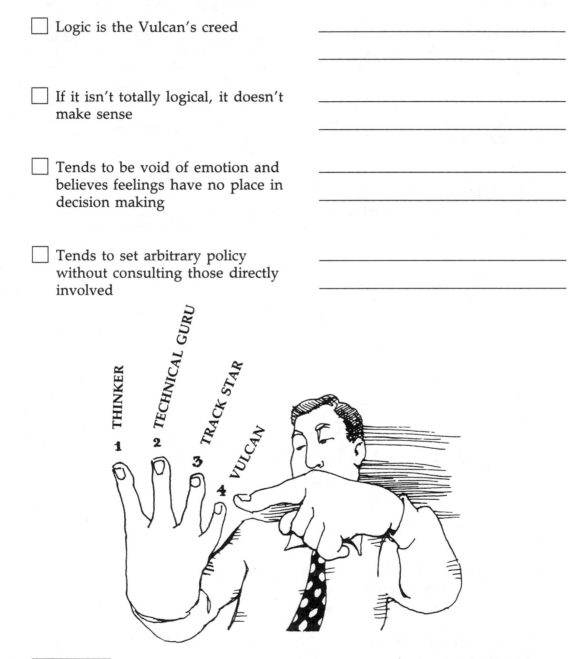

SUGGESTED RESPONSES TO A CLOSER LOOK

Now take a moment to compare your recommendations for increased supervisory effectiveness with those of authors Davis and Lewey.

The Thinker

- **Set decision deadlines.**

  The thinker might even share the situation with a trusted colleague, asking for a reminder as the deadline draws near.

- **Learn to trust your gut.**

  Each person has two sides of his or her personality: the analytical and the intuitive. Thinkers must learn to trust the latter.

- **Increase risk-taking behavior.**

  By definition, all decisions have risks. Thinkers must ask, ''What's the worst thing that could happen if this decision is made?'' Then compare that with the consequences of not making any decision at all.

The Technical Guru

- **Redefine politics and power.**

  You need to redefine ''politics,'' in particular, so the word carries a positive connotation. The guru needs to see politics as a means for achieving organizational objectives through others and through resources that are not under his or her direct control.

- **Learn to network.**

  The guru needs to become a part of both internal and external networks by scheduling lunches, breaks and informal meetings. Chances are he or she will be a welcome resource. In turn the guru learns how to develop his or her own network.

- **Build a referent power base.**

  This simply means influencing people in an organization through interpersonal relationships and trust. Gurus should periodically audit their referent power base.

SUGGESTED RESPONSES TO A CLOSER LOOK (continued)

The Track Star

- **Seek out and compliment skills in others.**

  This is probably one of the easiest remedies. Track stars must remember that a key point in recognizing the skills of co-workers is to do so in public.

- **Look for collaborative assignments.**

  This will help develop a teamwork attitude, in addition to building a personal network. As time goes on, track stars will begin to believe the old adage that two heads are better than one.

- **Curb the appetite for competitive debate.**

  Some people argue for the sheer fun of argument. They thrive on it. Yet many don't share that belief and are hurt or offended by direct confrontation.

The Vulcan

- **Consider feelings as another data source.**

  Managers should enter feelings into the formula when making a decision. Vulcans should seek input from a trusted co-worker who is more in tune with how the people affected by decisions are likely to feel.

- **Learn to identify and disclose feelings.**

  In a given situation, Vulcans should seriously reflect on the feelings of the moment and make a point of telling others those feelings, good or bad.

- **Develop a feeling vocabulary.**

  Vulcans can add to their daily conversations phrases like ''I understand how you must feel'' and ''I'm happy for you.''

- **Acknowledge others' feelings through reflective skills.**

  When someone shares an experience with a Vulcan, that manager should equate it to a similar personal experience, then share those feelings.

PROACTIVE MANAGEMENT

Technical environments are often described as intense activity traps. Not only does the new technical supervisor have to meet the challenges of understanding other technical types, but he or she has to respond to rapid changes in technologies, organizational structures and the broader environment.

Our concern here is to assure that you not fall victim to only reactive behaviors, but rather to encourage you to make proactive responses. You will then be modeling the very behaviors you are seeking in others.

Exercise: Proactive Supervision

Select the two issues that affect your role as a technical supervisor. List two proactive approaches you can take to resolve conflict.

ISSUES:

☐ Importance of people skills

☐ Shifting workplace values

☐ Changing demographics

☐ Project and matrix management methodologies

☐ Changing organizational structures and concepts

☐ Demand for new technical skills

☐ Process and equipment technology improvements

☐ Computing and information systems improvements

☐ Regulating changes

☐ National and organizational political scenarios

Issue

1. _____

2. _____

Proactive Response

a. _____

b. _____

a. _____

b. _____

TECHNICAL SUPERVISORS' TRANSITION LESSONS

Experience shows that one of the best ways to develop your competencies (knowledge, skills and attitudes) as a technical supervisor is by finding a coach or mentor who will take you under his or her wing and help you develop.

As you seek to identify your mentor, we would like to take the liberty of providing you with several of ours. You will have the opportunity to meet four individuals at the end of each section. They will provide advice specifically relevant to that section. After they provide you with their advice, we will encourage you to respond by answering the two questions that relate their experiences to yours.

Technical Supervisor #1

Name: Taylor

Current Job: Group Leader

Educational Background and Degrees: BA, Mathematics

Technical Specialty and Experience: Data Communication Systems, Data Communication Protocols

- *Why did you take your first technical supervising position?*

  I wanted to be "in charge"; I wanted more responsibility; I wanted to direct, rather than do (and thought I would be better than any of the other likely candidates).

- *Did you have any difficulty in making the transition from being a technical expert to supervising the work of other technical professionals?*

  It was difficult to learn to trust the technical work of others, to create a job description for myself, to learn how to translate sponsor requests into jobs for my staff (including defining schedules and an appropriate level of support).

- *What recommendations would you give to a technical expert making that first transition to technical supervisor?*

  Establish your position and let your staff know what you expect and how you view your role as soon as possible. Make sure that they all understand their tasks (and that you understand what they're doing).

Technical Supervisor #2

Name: Caton

Current Job: Director, Program Development

Educational Background and Degrees: BS, General Engineering; MBA; MS, Contract and Acquisition Management

Technical Specialty and Experience: Electronic Warfare Systems Engineering

- *Why did you take your first technical supervising position?*

Career growth.

- *Did you have any difficulty in making the transition from being a technical expert to supervising the work of other technical professionals?*

I occasionally felt inadequate when I was supervising technical staff outside of my technical specialty, such as in a design discipline.

- *What recommendations would you make to a technical expert making that first transition to technical supervisor?*

Seek formal training for your new role. It will build your confidence, let you know what to expect and speed up your goal performance.

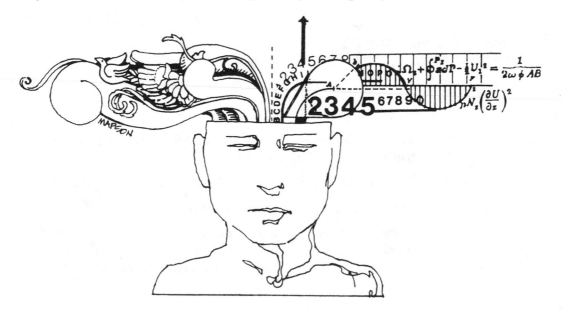

TECHNICAL SUPERVISORS' TRANSITION LESSONS (continued)

Technical Supervisor #3

Name: Pat

Current Job: Principal Investigator

Educational Background and Degrees: BA, Chemistry; MS, Biochemistry; Ph.D., Nutritional Biochemistry; MAS, Management

Technical Specialty and Experience: Intermediate metabolism, sulfur metabolism, obesity.

- *Why did you take your first technical supervising position?*

  I wanted more room for advancement and higher salary potential.

- *Did you have any difficulty in making the transition from being a technical expert to supervising the work of other technical professionals?*

  Yes, I wasn't quite sure what I was getting into.

- *What recommendations would you make to a technical expert making that first transition to technical supervisor?*

  Technical people often don't have people skills. Develop communication skills and ways to get cooperation from others without issuing orders.

Technical Supervisor #4

Name: Shawn

Current Job: Chief, Space Intelligence

Educational Background and Degrees: Two years college; Extensive training and education in the Army; BS, Business Management

Technical Specialty and Experience: Space and Missile Telemetry Systems

- *Why did you take your first technical supervising position?*

  As I moved up in grade and from a career standpoint, it was in my best interest to take the position of my immediate boss when he retired. I also had the long-term corporate knowledge within my organization to help with future operations.

- *Did you have any difficulty in making the transition from being a technical expert to supervising the work of other technical professionals?*

Not really. I found that many of my management courses helped, but so did my association with my past supervisor, who led by example and had the respect of all of his workforce. I found that if you treat people in an adult manner and give them the respect you would like, they will perform. Even when I had problem employees, I made them understand that their lower-than-normal annual rating would be to their benefit in the long run, and we would work together to solve their problems both on and off the job.

- *What recommendations would you make to a technical expert making that first transition to technical supervisor?*

To make an effective transition, NEVER, NEVER, NEVER arrive and say this is the way we are going to do things now. ALWAYS, ALWAYS, ALWAYS keep your ears open first and find out the pros and cons of the organization and what the workforce wants or needs from you, and then implement the changes that are needed. Explain your ideas and keep people informed. There is nothing worse than a rumor mill.

Lessons Learned

1. What are the similarities between your transition experience and those of our supervisors'? _____

_____

2. Did any of their recommendations have special value for you? _____

_____

We will meet these experts again in each section of the workbook.

Technical Supervisor Questionnaire

Please complete and return the questionnaire appearing at the end of this book. This will not only help us improve the relevance of future editions of this book, but also help you meet your future training and development needs.

PART

II

Communication:
Skills for Technical
Supervisors

COMMUNICATION CHALLENGES FACING TECHNICAL SUPERVISORS

Perhaps the most difficult obstacle the new technical supervisor needs to surmount is the immediate acquisition of communication skills. Three very real challenges must be faced and met. Which do you find most difficult?

► **Understanding Your Style of Communication**

Your educational and career choice, probably rooted to childhood interests, reflects a preference for quantitative reasoning, critical thinking and, often, working alone. It is no surprise, or fault of anyone, that this set of aptitudes, while compatible with the role of technologist, might not include the skills needed to work with others in the social situations demanded of a supervisor. The move from individual technical contributor to coordinator of the work of others will quickly stretch your communication comfort zone.

► **Meeting Interpersonal Communication Demands**

Global economies, changing organizational structures and new technologies have created new communication environments. Individual contributors are now part of team and project activities. Technical supervisors, and the very technical experts they supervise, may have dual reporting lines. Such matrix structures provide technical direction from one source and administrative direction from another. And, of course, mergers, acquisitions, downsizing, "right-sizing" and process re-engineering add other communication demands.

► **Developing Situational Communication Strategies**

New technical supervisors suddenly find themselves in an intense political arena. Dealing with competition for resources, sudden and frequent change, confusing and overlapping responsibilities and conflicting goals and agendas requires the application of communication strategies and tactics beyond their previous study and experience.

Knowing and flexing your communication style, meeting the intense interpersonal communication needs of technical environments, and employing effective situational communication strategies are critical technical supervisor skills. Here are some specific approaches for each challenge.

CHALLENGE #1: UNDERSTANDING YOUR STYLE OF COMMUNICATION

As a technical expert you may not have been introduced to the concept of personal style. The last section suggested that each of us has his or her own behavioral pattern—the distinct way that we think, feel and act.

Here is a brief overview of the functions of behavior associated with the four main styles.

STYLE	FUNCTION
Intuitor	Conceiving, projecting, inducing
Thinker	Analyzing, ordering in logical fashion
Feeler	Relating to and understanding experience through emotional reactions and responses to feelings
Sensor	Experiencing mainly on the basis of one's own sensory perceptions

Knowing our primary and secondary styles can help us understand how we experience things and how we behave. The goal for technical supervisors, of course, is understanding their personal and communication style and to develop the ability to "flex" their style to meet the demands of other people and situations.

TECHNICAL SUPERVISORS AND COMMUNICATION STYLES

People who select technical disciplines tend to be Thinkers and Sensors as opposed to Intuitors and Feelers.

How could a Thinker or Sensor improve his or her communication style?

_____

_____

_____

_____

What effective behaviors can be learned from Intuitors and Feelers?

_____

_____

_____

_____

The following page, containing a list of effective and ineffective characteristics, may be helpful in answering these questions.

Which words describe your behavior(s)?

_____

_____

_____

_____

Do you see areas for improvement?

_____

_____

_____

_____

CHALLENGE #1 (continued)

Communication Characteristics

	Effective	Ineffective
Intuitor	original	unrealistic
	imaginative	"far-out"
	creative	fantasy-bound
	broad-gauged	scattered
	charismatic	devious
	idealistic	out-of-touch
	intellectually tenacious	dogmatic
	ideological	impractical
Thinker	effective communicator	verbose
	deliberate	indecisive
	prudent	overly cautious
	weighs alternatives	overanalyzes
	stabilizing	unemotional
	objective	nondynamic
	rational	controlled and controlling
	analytical	overly serious, rigid

	Effective	**Ineffective**
Feeler	spontaneous	impulsive
	persuasive	manipulative
	empathetic	overpersonalizes
	grasps traditional values	sentimental
	probing	postponing
	introspective	guilt-ridden
	draws out feelings	stirs up conflict
	loyal	subjective
Sensor	pragmatic	doesn't look ahead
	assertive, directional	status seeking, self-involved
	result-oriented	acts first, then thinks
	competitive	domineering
	confident	arrogant
	objective; bases opinions on what is actually seen	lacks trust in others

The above is used with permission from DBM Publishing, a division of DBM, Inc. I-Speak Your Language,® A Survey of Personal Styles Manual. © 1972, 1993, p. 24.

From Technical Specialist to Supervisor

CHALLENGE #2: MEETING INTERPERSONAL COMMUNICATION DEMANDS

Technical supervisors spend most of their time communicating on an interpersonal level. This involves not only the *exchange of messages*, but equally important to your effectiveness, the *development of a relationship based* on the effect of those messages.

An earlier section suggested that you must constantly balance your *task-orientation* with *people-orientation*. Effective interpersonal communication allows you to do just that.

While much has been written about the importance of effective communication, technical supervisors need recommendations just for them. They have specific needs that go beyond the basics—needs unique to technical supervisors managing technical experts.

Dale E. Jackson's excellent book *Interpersonal Communication for Technically Trained Managers: A Guide to Skills and Techniques* is just for you. We have taken the liberty, with the author's permission, of presenting an Interpersonal Communication Resource Kit based on material appearing in this book.

Interpersonal Communication Resource Kit

Exercise

1. Please identify two individuals (work-related) with whom you would like to improve your interpersonal communication skills.

2. Then review the suggested communication techniques provided by Dale E. Jackson that follow and select the specific techniques that are most appropriate. Write them in the space provided.

3. Review your tactics with a colleague before trying them.

4. Actually use these techniques with the people you targeted for practice.

5. Evaluate their effectiveness and try again.

Individual Targeted for Practice

1. _____

2. _____

Communication Techniques

a. _____

   _____

b. _____

   _____

c. _____

   _____

a. _____

   _____

b. _____

   _____

c. _____

   _____

CHALLENGE #2 (continued)

Suggested Techniques

1. **Each part of a manger's job has its own set of communication skills.** These include:

- Communicate to help the group of people who report to you meet the needs of the organization or project.

- Communicate to meet the needs of the individual members of the group.

- Communicate as an individual to help meet the needs of the project.

- Communicate your needs as an individual.

2. **Effective communicators "stay on top of the mountain" through assertive techniques.** This is defined as:

- To maintain a right or claim by words or by action.

- To insist on being recognized.

- To state positively, to affirm, to allege, to declare.

3. **Active listening, listening according to the needs of the other person, significantly enhances interpersonal communication.** In this mode you should be able to "report" back to the other individual three things:

- The facts as the other person described them.

- A word or two that describes how the other person seems to feel.

- The use of the second-person pronoun "you" to reface your description of the other person's feelings (optional).

4. **Most of the information others receive from you comes through nonverbal channels.** Mastering your nonverbal signals will increase the accuracy of your listener's understanding of what you are saying.

5. **Managers have emotions and feelings.** You can manage your emotions by expressing them (self-disclosure). When you disclose yourself, make three things very clear to the other person:

- The act you are referring to.

- How you really feel about it, not how you think you should feel about it.

- The effects of that act on your job, the project, the department or the situation in general. Be as quantitative as your knowledge of the facts will permit.

6. **The better you can communicate, the more you will realize that communication is never complete and never accurate.** You might also realize that it never happens the way you think it does.

7. **Present and inform; you won't need to persuade.** Strategically choose from these courses of action:

- Persuade—moving another person to do something or to accept a belief.

- Present—submitting for the other person's consideration. This offers the other person a chance to change his or her store of knowledge, but does not try to make him or her change what he or she says or does.

- Inform—giving someone information he or she did not know before.

8. **Those whom you will persuade to change their actions will do so only when they are convinced that you recognize their personal importance and ability.**

Remember, when you are trying to persuade someone over whom you have little influence and no authority, that your most effective skill is active listening.

CHALLENGE #2 (continued)

9. **Most of the decision-making process is communication.** The most valuable skills are assertion, active listening, nonverbal communication and the exchange of facts. These communication skills will do more than increase your chance of making good decisions.

10. **The more communication, the better the performance planning.** The supervisor can significantly improve this critical and difficult process by:

- Appreciating the importance of the greeting, making small talk and establishing rapport.

- Seeking a workable compromise as appraiser and appraisee plan together for future performance.

- Listening for feelings as well as facts.

- Professionally expressing pleasure and displeasure.

- Avoiding nonverbal giveaways and noticing nonverbal messages from the appraisee.

- Emphasizing facts and feedback.

- Clearly informing the other party of the performance alternatives that are open to him or her.

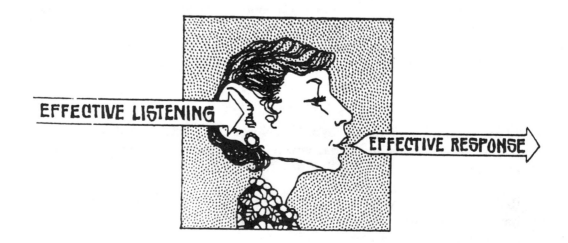

EFFECTIVE LISTENING

EFFECTIVE RESPONSE

Based on material by Dale E. Jackson. *Interpersonal Communication for Technically Trained Managers: A Guide to Skills and Techniques.* New York: Quorum Books. 1988.

CHALLENGE #3: DEVELOPING SITUATIONAL COMMUNICATION STRATEGIES

Technical supervisors are highly motivated people looking for more responsibility, authority and challenge.

As technical experts, they could communicate technical information, diplomatically provide advice to their team members, and share ideas, understanding both facts and feelings.

Now as technical supervisors, they find themselves thrust into new communication arenas. They often have to balance the concerns of individuals and projects (people and tasks), reconcile conflicts between individuals and groups, and communicate technical information to nontechnical senior management.

And if they move up to the role of technical manager, they will have to develop more sophisticated communication, negotiation and influence skills to sell ideas in competitive environments.

SITUATIONAL COMMUNICATION STRATEGIES

Telling, Selling, Consulting or Joining

Technical experts' communication is influenced by years of rigorous academic study, a self-imposed drive for excellence and achievement, and intense periods of working alone. As a result, they often rely too heavily on "telling" or "selling" instead of the underused "consulting" and "joining" styles of communication.

Each of these four styles, originally presented in *Supervising Technical and Professional People*, by Martin Broadwell and Ruth Sizemore House, is valuable in the right situation. The proactive technical supervisor needs to learn to use each type (a strategy) and its specific actions (tactics) to his or her advantage.

Four Communication Models

Identify a specific work-related communication situation where you could use each style effectively. Discuss your application with a co-worker or your manager, to critique your effectiveness.

1. Telling

Used when a task is either very difficult or very simple with predictable outcomes. It is a step-by-step explanation of what you expect. Sometimes a checklist of "what to do" and "how to do it" is effective.

Five Steps for "Telling":

- Spell out your expectations
- Acknowledge what is going well now
- Identify what is not going well now
- Point out the advantages of doing things the way you want
- Spell out the consequences of noncompliance

Application: _____

_____

2. Selling

Used, more likely, when other factors—the personalities involved, the organizational conditions or the urgency of the task—take precedence. The decision to use the selling approach has little to do with the complexity of the task.

Suggestions for Using the "Selling" Model:

- Potential colleagues may withhold support for projects they don't originate
- Input is required before the situation becomes urgent
- It requires a thorough explanation of the benefits of the idea
- The features of the new procedures need to be spelled out

Application: _____

_____

3. Consulting

Requires input from staff to get a clear picture of the situation. Consulting is a good approach when your staff has a specialized knowledge of the situation that you may not. It allows you to receive maximum input, while remaining in control of related decisions.

An Ideal "Consulting" Model Follows These Steps:

- Check each person's understanding of the problem
- Clarify each person's role in arriving at a solution
- Develop criteria for a good solution
- Encourage data and idea sharing
- Summarize each person's ideas to his or her satisfaction
- Evaluate
- Decide

Application: _____

_____

THE "JOINING" COMMUNICATION MODEL

CHALLENGE #3 (continued)

4. Joining

Supports the belief that a decision can best be made by the whole group. While the supervisor is ultimately responsible for the final decision, he or she should recognize that there are times when an informed, technical decision can best be made by the the technical experts themselves.

In this interactive approach, the supervisor helps manage the flow of information, helps siphon off emotional distraction and helps clarify.

The "Joining" Model Follows Five Basic Steps:

- Check everyone's understanding of the problem.
- Clarify each person's role in making the decision.
- Work with the group to develop criteria for a good decision.
- Encourage data and idea sharing.
- Summarize each person's ideas to his or her satisfaction.

Application: _____

_____

Adopted, with permission, from *Supervising Technical and Professional People* by Ruth Sizemore House and Martin Broadwell. Copyright © 1986 by John Wiley and Sons, Inc.

APPLYING COMMUNICATION MODELS

Effective technical supervisors increase their communication effectiveness by continually expanding their style, strategies and tactics. On the basis of the previous exercise, how would you respond to the following statements?

The approach I *use most* is _____

The approach I *use least* is _____

Review: Telling, Selling, Consulting or Joining

As a communication strategist, I would use the following approach, or *combination* of approaches, in the situations listed below:

Situation	Interaction Models
1. Giving and receiving positive feedback:	_____ _____
2. Handling poor performance through constructive feedback:	_____ _____
3. Gaining cooperation and commitment from my immediate work group:	_____ _____
4. Communicating to nonreporting people outside my immediate work group:	_____ _____
5. Communicating a shift in technical priorities:	_____ _____

TECHNICAL SUPERVISORS' COMMUNICATION LESSONS

Earlier our experienced technical supervisors made recommendations for making the transition from technical expert to supervisor. Those supervisors are back again with advice about communication skills for technical supervisors. After you review their advice, please answer two questions relating their experiences to yours.

Technical Supervisor #1: Taylor, Group Leader

1. *What specific challenges did you experience in communicating to technical professionals?*

   Trying to understand both the sponsor needs and the technical aspects of a particular job. It was hard to communicate why we should take a certain direction when it wasn't the best technical choice.

2. *What specific recommendations would you make to help other technical professionals develop their communication skills?*

   Practice, practice, practice. Take classes in writing, briefing and other communication skills. Ask for feedback from your bosses and friends. Learn to listen before speaking; learn to find out what needs to be done; and learn to summarize and get commitment at the end of a conversation.

Technical Supervisor #2: Caton, Director, Program Development

1. *What specific challenges did you experience in communicating to technical professionals?*

   Supervisors find themselves directing and communicating with multiple disciplines even though they may not possess specific technical jargon.

2. *What specific recommendations would you make to help other technical professionals develop their communication skills?*

   - Attend proposal development seminars and read about others' experiences.

   - Attend a workshop on making oral presentations.

   - Develop your writing skills.

Technical Supervisor #3: Pat, Principal Investigator

1. *What specific challenges did you experience in communicating to technical professionals?*

   As a rather "quiet person," I found I had to stretch my comfort zone to initiate conversations with staff.

2. *What specific recommendations would you make to help other technical professionals develop their communication skills?*

   Try to model the very behaviors you are encouraging them to try out. Encourage participation in communication workshops and seminars offered by local colleges.

Technical Supervisor #4: Shawn, Chief, Space Intelligence

1. *What specific challenges did you experience in communicating to technical professionals?*

   Never try to "snow" anyone! In dealing with highly skilled and professional people, you cannot put up a false front. If you do not know something, say so; people will understand this and forgive, but to muddy the communications by side-stepping issues will always lead to mistrust. It will lower your credibility.

2. *What specific recommendations would you make to help other technical professionals develop their communication skills?*

   Often the best employee in a technical line doesn't want anything to do with standing up in front of a group and presenting a briefing. While many can write well, they often lack verbal skills. This can lead to stage fright. The best remedy is experience. A briefing skills course would help, and practice in front of small groups will build confidence.

TECHNICAL SUPERVISORS' COMMUNICATION LESSONS (continued)

Lessons Learned

1. What are the similarities between your transitional experience and those of our supervisors?

_____

_____

_____

_____

_____

2. Did any of their recommendations have special value for you?

_____

_____

_____

_____

_____

(Keep in mind that we will meet them again in each section of this book.)

P A R T

III

Motivation:
Creating Incentives

MOTIVATIONAL ISSUES

A curious "motivational paradox" exists for technical supervisors. On one hand, individuals and organizations recognize the importance of high-quality environments that provide incentives for people to flourish. Many books—some mentioned in the bibliography—encourage supervisors to empower and motivate people, and manage for commitment, performance and productivity.

However, the workplace (particularly technology-driven organizations) is often chaotic, changing and fiercely competitive. In this organizational environment, the people side of the enterprise, the creating and sustaining of incentives for people to flourish, is too often neglected.

Your role as technical supervisor quickly emerges as the critically important "motivational linking pin." Since your motivational skills will probably be stretched and exhausted, we are giving you tools and techniques to work with now.

Understanding Motivational Issues

We would also like you to appreciate and be prepared to address the following motivational issues:

► **As a technical supervisor, you are a manager of performance.**

And performance managers know how to define expectations and set goals, delegate, train, coach, counsel and appraise performance. These skills all enhance your motivational effectiveness.

► **Your efforts to motivate your own staff fit into the broader human resource management continuum.**

Ideally, the supervisor and the organization integrate recruiting, selecting, managing, motivating and retaining employees. Talented technical professionals have high expectations; if you and your organization cannot meet their needs, others will.

MOTIVATIONAL ISSUES (continued)

▶ **A curious technical supervisor counterpoint is in progress.**

At the same time an organization, or an entire industry, is seeking to empower individuals, build employee loyalty and productivity, and manage upward for commitment, a process of mergers, acquisitions and right-sizing may be under way. Realistically, you may be consciously working to motivate your people as they are facing the three ''Ds'': downsizing, dismissal and dismantling.

▶ **Technical environments are complicated socio-technical systems.**

The needs of people, their organization and technology are at times in conflict.

As a technical supervisor, you face constant challenges. Which of these can you identify with?

- New technologies require a high degree of commitment and autonomy on the part of technical professionals. These may conflict with the bureaucratic techno-structure.

- New and rapidly changing technologies disturb long-established boundaries between jobs and skills and between operation and maintenance.

- New technologies and complex technical environments place a burden on the technical supervisor to establish a social system and motivational alternatives to fully implement the technology.

▶ **As a technical supervisor, you should continually assess and develop your technical experts' competence and motivation.**

Competence, as we previously defined, reflects the understanding of what to do. It is their ''can do'' ability. Motivation is their internally driven ''will do'' ability. In the next section on delegation, these ''can do'' and ''will do'' factors will influence how you monitor performance.

MOTIVATIONAL THEORIES

While we will quickly focus on the unique motivational needs of technical experts and their supervisors, we can learn some quick lessons from the "tried and true." In fact, according to the Oxford Dictionary of English, one definition of "new" is "rediscovering the old."

Two motivational theories present concepts relevant to motivating technical professionals. Which ideas do you find most relevant?

1. Need for Achievement

David C. McClelland, writing in *The Achieving Society* in 1961, suggests that some people have a compelling need to achieve simply for the sake of achieving rather than for whatever benefits or symbols of success might follow high achievement.

High achievers are trail blazers and innovators. They thrive on increasingly greater responsibility; they impose their own demanding standards of excellence. They have the desire to be the best at something.

How do you motivate your high achievers? Take a moment to identify and describe your current motivators for two such technical professionals.

High Achiever #1	**High Achiever #2**
Motivators I Employ:	*Motivators I Employ:*
• _____	• _____
• _____	• _____

Two other needs for understanding human behavior have been identified—*the need for affiliation* and *the need for power*.

MOTIVATIONAL THEORIES (continued)

2. Motivation-Hygiene Theory

Frederick Hertzberg's book *The Motivation to Work,* published in 1959, presents another theory relevant to motivating technical experts. He suggests that a manager must manage the job environment to control performance and turnover.

More specifically, his major conclusion is that there are two sets of factors into which motivational aspects of jobs can be placed—satisfiers and dissatisfiers. Too often managers assume that the following "dissatisfiers" will motivate technical experts. Ironically, many current human resource management systems are still anchored to these industrial-age tools.

Dissatisfiers

This set of factors in the workplace is composed of all those things which, when absent, would create dissatisfaction. Hertzberg calls these "hygiene factors." They include:

- Acceptable company policies and rules.
- Tolerable management methods by the immediate supervisor.
- Equitable compensation.
- Congenial interpersonal relations with co-workers.
- Agreeable working conditions.

Satisfiers

The second set of factors in the job situation that Hertzberg describes corresponds to the needs found at the top of Abraham Maslow's hierarchy. These are the "true motivators" that appeal to the needs of people to grow and to develop to their full potential. These motivators include:

- A sense of achievement, or the knowledge of having done something worthwhile.
- Recognition, by persons whose opinion is valued, that one's work has merit.
- The satisfaction that comes from challenging work.
- A high degree of responsibility on the job.
- An opportunity for advancement, growth and development.

Discussion Questions

1. At which levels of need are technical professionals likely to operate?

   _____

   _____

2. How can managers use Hertzberg's theory to fill the needs of and motivate their employees?

   _____

   _____

3. Where do you fit into Hertzberg's levels compared to the people you supervise? Are both technical professionals and supervisors motivated in the same way?

   _____

   _____

MOTIVATIONAL BASICS

Our emphasis is on addressing the unique demands of supervising technical experts in technology-driven environments. However, our motivational efforts should not overlook the basics. Take a moment to review the following list of motivational factors originally published by the Training Resource Company.

Basic Motivational Factors

1. Clear job objectives

2. Performance standards that challenge

3. Decision-making authority

4. Opportunity to solve own problems

5. Opportunity to check own work quality

6. Opportunity to complete whole work untis

7. Variety of job tasks

8. Knowledge of the job's contribution to final product/service

9. Knowledge of the job's relationship to other company operations

10. Access to information needed to do the job

11. Access to information about anticipated changes

12. Awareness of superior's schedule, activities (where appropriate)

13. Access to product information

14. Access to market information

15. Direct communication from manager (i.e., more face-to-face contact than memos or notices)

16. Positive performance feedback from manager

17. Constructive criticism from manager

UNIQUE MOTIVATIONAL NEEDS OF TECHNICAL EPERTS

Over the past few years much has been written about the unique challenge of motivating and managing technical professionals and the unique motivational needs technical experts have.

What Characterizes Technical Experts?

The following list describes some of the research-documented behaviors of technical professionals from "A–Z." Can you help the author find behaviors for H, J and X?

A Autonomy demanded

B Big-picture perspective lacking

C Calculated risk-taker

D Development of career is critical

E Evaluation and integrity of ideas paramount

F Freedom from constraints demanded

G Guidance in setting goals and expectations required

H _____

I Interaction with others a low need

J _____

K Knowledge is king

L Loyal to their technology and profession before the organization

M Manager's support and political cushioning expected

O Organizationally disengaged

P Professional growth an extraordinarily high need

Q Question and challenge management

R Respect the technical

S Specialized to a high degree

T Technologic innovators

U Underestimate time frames

V Personal values must be respected

W Work environment demands are high

X _____

Y Often young and double-degreed

Z Zealous about new technologies

MATCHING REWARDS TO PROFESSIONAL CHARACTERISTICS

How to Really Motivate Technical Experts

Dr. Von Glinow, author of *The New Professionals,* suggests that the real way to motivate technical professionals is by specifically creating a "new motivational schema"—incentives matched to the individual values and beliefs of the professionals. Interestingly, this motivational model closely resembles the characteristics of a professional association or university. (Research also indicates that technical experts have more loyalty to their academic discipline and alma mater than to their organization).

Characteristics	Suggested Motivators
1. *Expertise*	• Provide for the maintenance and growth of professional skills over time to avoid obsolescence
	• Quality of facilities (space, privacy, equipment) and facilitative support services
	• Leaves of absence, seminars, management training, sabbatical (15–20% of base salary)
	• Development counseling (career-shifting)
2. *Ethics*	• Reduce conflicting demands from colleagues, superiors and clients
	• Allow information sharing with referents outside the firm (publication)
	• Provide recognition for technical and scientific contributions
3. *Collegial Maintenance of Standards*	• Peer and group evaluation and appraisals
	• Establishment of appropriate evaluation criteria

4. *Autonomy*

- Reduce the network rules and regulations for professionals

- Protective structures (professional liaisons)

- Use of time and funds for personal goals

- Removal from physical plant to smaller "garage" environments of "independent business units" to induce creativity and innovation

- Freedom to select tasks and projects and to implement one's own ideas; flexible working hours

- Delete "tight" supervisory controls

- Delegate decision-making authority

5. *Commitment to Calling*

- Establish alternative promotional ladders to allow technical professionals to remain in their specialties (with parity)

- Career assessment and development

6. *External Referents and Identification*

- Encourage attendance at professional meetings and research presentations

- Publish and take out patents and copyrights under professional's own name

From Technical Specialist to Supervisor

Exercise: Find the Motivational Match

You recently had the opportunity to hire three new technical experts to be assigned to three diverse projects. From past experience you have learned that finding the best *motivational match* is as important as balancing *technical skills*.

Projects

Project A:

Long-Term Maintenance Operation. A single high-performing product account for a large part of the company's income. An ongoing research-and-development effort, as well as a rigorous quality assurance program, is needed to maintain your market share as the organization attempts to bring new products to market. This technical expert needs to make a two-year commitment to this project.

Project B:

Matrix Team Design. Recent organizational changes have resulted in a compression of management levels, greater emphasis on cross-functional teams and a more effective charge-back system for direct and indirect costs. This technical expert will have to work with a wide variety of people in highly accountable and changing circumstances.

Project C:

Start-Up Initiative. Rapidly changing market conditions have forced your organization to bring a new product to market prematurely. A special technical expert team has been assembled to accelerate research and the manufacturing processes. Once this is completed (hopefully within four to six months) the team will be assigned to another equally challenging project.

Your first hour-long meeting with your new technical experts revealed the following information. Which project assignment would make the most effective motivational match? (Assume that each individual has the appropriate technical skills.)

The Technical Experts

Blair scored very strong as a **sensor** on the personal style survey. She is results-oriented, assertive, directional and objective. In discussion, Blair indicated a desire to be challenged, a desire to have direct communication with multiple levels of management and a preference for a variety of tasks.

Harib scored very strong as an **intuitor** on the personal style survey. Words like "original," "creative," "broad-gauged," "charismatic" and "intellectually persistent" characterized Harib's personal style. His past employers identified these work preferences: likes a variety of job tasks, seeks knowledge of job's relationship to other company's operations, needs access to information about anticipated changes.

Kim Fu's behavior is described as deliberative, prudent, stabilizing, analytical and objective. This characterizes the behavior of **thinkers**. Kim Fu seeks opportunities to solve his own problems, access to information he needs to do the job, and clear job objectives.

Motivational Match	Technical Expert	Reason Chosen
Project A	_____	_____
Project B	_____	_____
Project C	_____	_____

Answers:

Project A, Kim Fu; *Project B,* Harib; *Project C,* Blair. Information used to create cases was selected from "Motivational Tasks" and "Characteristics Associated With Communication Style."

WHAT MOTIVATES TECHNICAL SUPERVISORS?

As a technical supervisor, you are caught in the middle. Not only are you meeting all of the challenges of supervising technical experts, but you are also responding to the expectations of your peers and managers. But how about you? Who is taking care of your needs?

Effective technical supervisors have a healthy self-interest. They take care of meeting their own motivational needs.

Four Types of High-Tech Managers
(And What Motivates Them)

Each of the following managers has his or her own strengths and weaknesses. The positive side is more productive and flexible, while the negative side is more defensive and rigid. You will gain some motivational insights if you identify yourself as one or more of these types.

Type #1: Craftspeople

Craftspeople value making, building and designing high-quality computer systems. They tend to be responsible, work-oriented, self-contained and prudently conservative. Craftspeople fit easily into a system of masters and apprentices. As leaders, they tend toward perfectionism. They seek one best way to do things, and find it difficult to delegate. They want to control the whole process, to infuse it with their high standards.

Craftspeople want to make money. Yet they are motivated even more by the problem to be solved, the challenge of the work itself and the satisfaction of creating something of quality. Many craftspeople belong to a larger category that can be called experts. They fit into specialized roles in a hierarchy.

But as markets, technology and employees' values change, their negative traits emerge more intensely. This is especially the case for craftspeople-experts in leadership positions. Their emphasis on personal control and ''one best way to do things'' limits their ability to make use of their employees' knowledge and turns off the new generation.

Type #2: Jungle Fighters

Jungle fighters are bold and entrepreneurial. They value survival skills and power. At their best, like the lion, they are defenders who protect their workplace families and uphold organizational values. Protectors at the top can create freedom for front line employees, but jungle fighters at middle levels resist sharing power and block the open exchange of information.

Type #3: Company Men and Women

Company men and women are a subcategory of people whose main satisfaction at work comes from helping people. Company people value harmony, cooperation and identification with the organization. They are other-directed careerists who climb the corporate ladder by making themselves useful to bosses. They flourished in the age of the rapid growth of wealthy American corporations. Typical company people are from large families and adapt to the corporation as if it were a new family, mediating conflicting demands for the good of all. At best, they are helpful institutional loyalists who support leadership and defend corporate values. At worst, their drive for consensus and fear of conflict drags the organization toward mediocrity; and their drive for status makes them turf-oriented bureaucrats. As corporations struggle to become lean and competitive, the negative side of company people is fueled by fear of the future and by confusion about their roles. To survive, they must become entrepreneurs, facilitators and educators.

READ ON . . .

WHAT MOTIVATES TECHNICAL SUPERVISORS? (continued)

Type #4: Games Players

Games players are highly competitive people who love change and want to influence its course. They like to take calculated risks and are fascinated by technique and new methods. They see developing projects, human relationships and their own careers in terms of options and possibilities, as if they were games. Their characters are collections of near-paradoxes understood in terms of adaptation to the needs of the business. They are detached and playful, and compulsively driven to succeed—team players trying to be superstars and team leaders who often rebel against bureaucratic hierarchy. They are fair and unprejudiced, contemptuous of weakness, tough and dominating, yet not destructive.

At best, games players are innovators who motivate others with their enthusiasm and freedom from bureaucratic constraints. At worst, their dreams become manipulations and promises, and they are intolerant of those who are not as dedicated to their creative plans.

This material is based on an article appearing in *Research Management*, ''Motivating Technical People,'' by Michael Maccoby. January/February 1985, Vol 30. Reprinted with permission.

MOTIVATIONAL CHALLENGES FACING TECHNICAL SUPERVISORS

New technical supervisors have an extra challenge in motivating technical experts. Several obstacles are influenced by the broader organizational and technological environment. Still others become their own responsibility. Which do you find most difficult?

► **Overcoming Trouble Pockets**

Technology-driven organizations experience rapid change and stress. Interestingly, both organizations and people regress to less effective behaviors when under stress. Gerald M. Weinberg's excellent book *Becoming a Technical Leader* suggests that a simple, yet effective, way to characterize a person's approach to leadership is by classifying his or her actions as *motivational, organizational* or *innovative*. In order for a leadership style to be effective, there must be balance among all three. Do you and your organization address these issues?

► **Creating a Positive Climate**

Organizations tend to withhold positive feedback. A psychologist will quickly point out that "withholding engenders withholding." As a technical supervisor, you can enhance the immediate motivational climate of your technical miniculture by telling people more often that they are doing well.

► **Finding Incentives for Your Technical Team**

Technical supervisors should build teams. The efforts of individual technicians are channeled into complex technical projects that require team effort. Human resource management systems, however, have not quite caught up with this concept. Most systems still financially reward the technical achievements of individual contributors, and not the accomplishments of team effort.

► **Managing Change**

"Margins of excellence," "quality assurance" and "technical innovation" are all competitive characteristics of organizations that manage change effectively. The technical supervisor and his or her motivational skills are tested and stretched in this area.

Now look at several of these challenges in greater detail.

CHALLENGE #1: OVERCOMING TROUBLE POCKETS

Your role, and your organization's broader role, can generate an *unfavorable* or *favorable* motivational climate. More specifically, your actions can be classified, according to author Gerald Weinberg, as *motivational, organizational* or *innovational*. Do you and your organization compare favorably or unfavorably to the MOI model?

Unfavorable Motivational Conditions

| M: motivation |

Kill the motivation Make people feel that you do not appreciate change; discourage anything that people might enjoy doing for its own sake; do everything for them, so they won't feel the need to do things for themselves.

| O: organization |

Foster chaos Encourage such stiff competition that cooperation will be unthinkable; keep resources slightly below the necessary minimum; suppress information fo general value, or bury it in an avalanche of meaningless stacks of paper.

| I: ideas of innovation |

Suppress the flow of ideas Don't listen when you can criticize instead; give your own ideas first and loudest; punish those who offer suggestions; keep people from working together; and above all, tolerate no laughter.

Or you can turn this trouble pocket around and provide:

Favorable Environmental Conditions

| M: motivation |
The trophies or trouble, the push or pull that moves the people involved.

| O: organization |
The existing structure that enables the ideas to be worked through into practice.

| I: ideas or innovation |
The seeds, the image of what will become.

Target Your Improvement Goals

According to the MOI model, I need to improve *my effectiveness,* as *technical supervisor,* by:

_____

_____

_____

I would like to encourage the senior management to increase our *organizational effectiveness,* by:

_____

_____

_____

CHALLENGE #2: CREATING A POSITIVE CLIMATE

Employees do not receive enough positive feedback. As a technical supervisor, you can enhance the positive motivational climate of your work group by taking the initiative to address this issue.

Application Exercise: Enhancing Productivity, Quality and the Motivational Climate

1. Identify a technical professional you feel is already doing a good job, but has the potential to do better.

   _____

   _____

   _____

   _____

2. Briefly outline a script for a meeting with this person using suggestions presented in both this section, and in the communication section of the workbook, that you feel would be relevant to him or her.

   _____

   _____

   _____

   _____

3. Conduct a face-to-face meeting where you "motivate" the individual to build on previous success, and go the extra distance. Then seek feedback from the employee or an observer on your effectiveness. Their response was:

   _____

   _____

   _____

   _____

CHALLENGE #3: FINDING INCENTIVES FOR YOUR TECHNICAL TEAM

Many technology-driven organizations have a conflicting agenda. Their mission encourages team activities, yet the performance appraisal system rewards individual technical achievement. Your challenge as a technical supervisor is to continue to find ways to motivate your technical team.

Where are you in the process of motivating a technical team?

► **You have effectively made the transition from technical expert to technical supervisor.**

Remember, earlier sections of this workbook described technical experts as analytical thinkers and quantitative reasoners with a great deal of cognitive ability.

As a technical supervisor, you have moved from a research-oriented perspective to an action-oriented role. Flexibility and adaptability are key passwords as you shift your focus. Your abilities to take the complex and make it simple, to maximize limited resources and to build and direct teams characterize your effectiveness as a technical supervisor.

► **Selecting and Supporting Technical Competence**

Motivation is the desire or willingness to do what is needed. Competence is the ability and understanding to do it. Critical technical assumptions for motivating technical teams are:

- You have selected or currently supervise an individual with the appropriate technical expertise;

- You are in a position to provide technical direction for or guide the tasks;

- You are adhering to clearly defined standards.

► **Motivating the Team Requires Leadership**

As a technical supervisor in a competitive technology-driven environment, you must develop leadership skills. Leaders are often described as those who take people places they would not have gone by themselves. Can you do this?

CHALLENGE #3 (continued)

It would be presumptuous, in such short space, to suggest that we can build your team. However, we can provide four suggestions to build team cooperation. How well are you currently doing in these areas?

- Notice how each employee works best: with close direction on a task; or with little direction on the task, yet with support in coordinating teamwork.

- Distinguish between tasks that require close direction and those that do not.

- Identify organizational conditions that require close direction and those that do not.

- Be familiar with several interaction models that can be adapted to suit the employees' personalities and a given situation (presented in a previous section).

CHALLENGE #4: MANAGING CHANGE

Managing change is an increasingly more important part of the technical supervisor's role. How the leader deals with change will enhance or impede the motivational climate of the work environment.

Each of the following technical supervisors has a motivational opportunity to manage change. Recognizing that they are new to the organization, they have turned to you, their *coach* and *mentor*, to advise them on what course of action to take.

Exercise: Review each case and the accompanying suggestions for managing change and motivation.

Case One: Shift of Priorities

Chris heads up a department that has always had relatively stable working conditions, assignments to long-term projects and opportunities for technical experts to work alone for long periods. But Chris's company was recently acquired by a large international firm.

It has become quite clear that Chris's department will now have to deal with a rapid shift of priorities. The new password is short-term economic success instead of long-term technical excellence.

Case Two: Monotonous Work

The employees in Khalil's department have a reputation as the organization's technical mavericks. Individually and collectively they have distinguished themselves by finding technical solutions for difficult problems.

Deteriorating economic conditions have forced the organization to eliminate several less cost-effective departments. A wide variety of routine, rather monotonous maintenance work has been assigned to several departments. Despite improved economic conditions, the organization is reluctant to hire staff to take back this work. Khalil's "technical mavericks" are overworked and stressed. Even overtime pay has lost its impact.

Khalil has just returned from a meeting with his boss. His department has received another "monotonous work overload." He has been told clearly that what was originally a short-term fix is now a formal part of his department's assignments. Before meeting with his staff, he is stopping by your office to seek your guidance.

CHALLENGE #4 (continued)

Case Three: The Importance of Team Activities—Mixed Signals

Mustafa's organization has enthusiastically joined the quality-management movement. A variety of consultants, along with training and development programs, have stressed the importance of team efforts. New mission statements and corporate brochures and posters all dramatize this new team initiative.

But as a new supervisor, Mustafa faces a curious paradox. The broad corporate *human resource department* supports the team concept; your boss even sent you a memo instructing you to put a team in place within thirty days. However, the organization's *human resource management system* still clearly rewards the technical achievements of individual contributors.

You are returning from a meeting with your boss, who once again reminded you ''to get that team in place.'' She did not care to address the issue of conflicting rewards (the technical excellence of individual contributors versus the achievements of technical teams.) It is clear that you will have to do the best you can to reconcile this situation.

Mustafa has called you for advice. You are his formally appointed coach and mentor.

Managing Change to Improve Motivation

- Change, while tied to positive learning and growth, is not in itself good or bad. Only the results count.

- There must be a desired goal.

- Desire for change comes from some form of discomfort.

- The supervisor, as the agent of change, can often help the group identify discomfort and thus help them feel it.

- Sometimes an outsider can be useful in the change-management process of the organization.

- Participants in the process must buy in—they must own the problem and the solution. This results from participation.

- Change is best managed by a participation process.

- A starting condition must be established through measurement, and those measurements must be taken along the way to determine whether or not progress is being made.

- The change process must be reinforced by recognition of and reward for contributions to the process. This is basic—as basic as the concept of participation.

What guidance would you provide for managing change and improving motivation?

Case One: **Shift of Priorities**

I would advise Chris to:

_____

_____

Case Two: **Department Overloaded with Monotonous Work**

I would advise Khalil to:

_____

_____

Case Three: **The Importance of Team Activities—Mixed Signals**

I would advise Mustafa to:

_____

_____

TECHNICAL SUPERVISORS' MOTIVATION LESSONS

Several experienced technical supervisors have advised you on the transition and on communication.

They are back again, this time answering two questions relevant to motivation skills for technical supervisors. After you review their advice, respond to the questions relating their experiences to yours.

Technical Supervisor #1 Taylor, Group Leader

---

1. *What specific challenges did you experience in motivating technical professionals?*

   Realizing that different things motivate different people. What motivates me as a technical supervisor, and what prompted me to become a technical supervisor in the first place, is significantly different from what motivates my staff.

2. *What specific recommendations would you make to help other technical professionals develop their motivation skills?*

   Think about what motivates you. Learn about personality types and their differences. Don't rely on salary administration and formal promotions for rewards.

Technical Supervisor #2 Caton, Director, Program Development

---

1. *What specific challenges did you experience in motivating technical professionals?*

   Winning credibility as a new manager.

2. *What specific recommendations would you make to help other technical professionals develop their motivation skills?*

   Take your staff into your confidence, seek their advice, share as much as you can, be consistent, be fair, always treat everyone with dignity and listen.

Technical Supervisor #3 Pat, Principal Investigator

1. *What specific challenges did you experience in motivating technical professionals?*

Some problems came up because I was young and had little seniority at the company. My subordinates did not want to listen to me or accept me as their supervisor.

2. *What specific recommendations would you make to help other technical professionals develop their motivation skills?*

Understand your employees' perspective. They may not see the relationship between their ''meaningless'' task and the overall program. Give them a global view.

Technical Supervisor #4 Shawn, Chief, Space Intelligence

1. *What specific challenges did you experience in motivating technical professionals?*

When you allow artists to create, they do much better than when you ask for a picture of your dog over the fireplace. It is much the same with the technical professional; these individuals know their jobs and can be extremely creative when required. I find that when you provide the necessary equipment and point them in the direction you wish to go, these folks will do the rest.

2. *What specific recommendations would you make to help other technical professionals develop their motivation skills?*

You can order people to do a job, you can use your higher position to force people to do a job, or you can ask someone for a task to be completed and he or she does so out of loyalty to you and the organization. I think that when you are an upright, no-bull kind of manager and help your people do their jobs—not stand in their way—they will be motivated by your example.

TECHNICAL SUPERVISORS' MOTIVATION LESSONS (continued)

Lessons Learned

1. What are the similarities between the experiences you have had motivating employees and those of our supervisors?

_____

_____

_____

_____

_____

_____

2. Did any of their recommendations have special value?

_____

_____

_____

_____

_____

_____

P A R T

IV

Delegation:
Learning to Let Go

DELEGATION SKILLS OVERVIEW

Many technical supervisors—and even senior technical managers—confess to the frustration of delegation. Not only is it difficult to give work to others that you may enjoy doing yourself, but it is a final test of "letting go."

In reality, you are giving work to another person to do. Symbolically, you are recognizing that by delegating you are relinquishing your role as a technical expert. Here is the irony. The more effective you are at technical supervision, the further away you move from the role of technical expert.

► Technical supervision is a rather nonlinear process. In one given instance you may have to apply skills in communication, motivation and delegation concurrently.

► Many technical supervisory occurrences are spontaneous and informal. While in an ideal world it would be nice to plan, implement and control each occurrence of communication, motivation and delegation, the reality of the workplace requires you to "seize the moment." You must know what to do well in advance.

► Behaviors and effectiveness regress under pressure. It is not surprising that under these circumstances it is common for people and organizations to retreat to more comfortable behaviors.

► For instance, if your primary interactive approach is *telling* and *selling* and you have been working to develop secondary *consulting* and *joining* skills, you may very well lapse into telling and selling under pressure. This, as you will soon see, has strong implications for effective delegating.

► Delegation signals from senior management are often mixed. On one hand, senior management encourages empowerment, team building and risk-taking. And yet, when the going gets tough, unquestioned success, competitive positioning and return on investment may quickly become the "real determinants." This affects the technical supervisor's style.

► Avoid the tendency to snatch back. As a proactive supervisor, you understand the reality of a technical environment. Shifting priorities, new deadlines and conflicting signals may tempt you to "snatch back" previously delegated work. And while you may truly do it better and faster, each time you "snatch back," you reinforce an environment characterized by the bumper sticker "Why is your lack of planning my source of crisis?"

Quite simply, when you "let go," don't snatch back.

HOW WELL DO I DELEGATE?

Learn how well you delegate. This scale will help identify your strengths and determine where improvement would help. Circle the number that best describes you. The higher the number, the more the statement describes you. When you have finished, total the numbers circled in the space provided.

1. Each of my employees knows what I expect of her or him.

   7 6 5 4 3 2 1

2. I involve employees in goal setting, problem solving and productivity improvement.

   7 6 5 4 3 2 1

3. My personal emphasis is on planning, organizing, motivating and controlling, rather than on doing tasks others could do.

   7 6 5 4 3 2 1

4. When assigning work, I select the assignee thoughtfully.

   7 6 5 4 3 2 1

5. When a problem occurs on a project I have delegated, I give the employee a reasonable chance to work it out for him or herself.

   7 6 5 4 3 2 1

6. When I delegate work to employees, I brief them fully on the details with which I am familiar.

   7 6 5 4 3 2 1

7. I see delegation as one way to help employees develop their skills, and I assign work accordingly.

   7 6 5 4 3 2 1

8. I support and help employees in emergencies, but I do not permit them to leave work.

   7 6 5 4 3 2 1

9. When I assign work, I stress results, not how to accomplish them.   7 6 5 4 3 2 1

10. When I delegate a project, I make sure everyone concerned knows who is in charge.   7 6 5 4 3 2 1

11. When delegating work, I balance authority with need and experience.   7 6 5 4 3 2 1

12. I hold my employees responsible for results.   7 6 5 4 3 2 1

TOTAL _____

A score between 72 and 84 suggests you are on target. A score between 48 and 71 indicates you are getting by, but could improve. Anything below 48 means you need to make changes.

Symptoms of Poor Delegation

If you scored less than 50 on this exercise, you might want to spend extra time thinking about each statement and about how you can begin to improve your delegation skills.

Supervising others requires time. Effectiveness can always be heightened by "pulling back the lens" to observe the performance of their employees, their organization and even themselves. This is especially important in delegation. There are many symptoms of poor delegation. They can usually be seen in the work habits of the manager, the attitude of the employees or the productivity of the group.

Delegation Deficiencies Checklist

In the list below, check the symptoms that are visible in your organization.

☐ Deadlines are frequently missed.

☐ Some employees are much busier than others.

☐ The supervisor (me) is usually too busy to talk to employees.

☐ Employees are unsure of their authority.

☐ No one in the unit is ever ready for promotion.

☐ Employee decisions are often overruled.

☐ No one seems to know who is in charge of a project.

☐ The organization is plagued by slow decision making.

☐ The supervisor (me) never has time to visit employee work areas.

☐ Changes in plans and objectives are not passed on to employees who need to know.

☐ Employees are assigned tasks they can't handle without training.

☐ The supervisor (me) sometimes intervenes in a project or assignment without informing the employee.

☐ Employees frequently request transfers to other units.

☐ The communication flow is sporadic, incomplete and often too late.

☐ The supervisor (me) often takes work home and sometimes reschedules his or her vacation because of the work load.

☐ Talented employees are bored.

☐ The supervisor (me) insists all mail must first pass through his or her office.

If you checked more than one or two of these statements, you should look carefully at your delegation practices and ask yourself why these conditions exist.

Exercise: Common Barriers to Delegation

Ineffective delegators rationalize their inadequacies in various ways. They usually center around obstacles (natural or self-made) in themselves, in the characteristics of their employees, or in the situation itself. In the following list of attitudes, indicate those that affect your delegation practices by checking Yes. If they do not affect you, check No. Think about each statement carefully and be completely honest.

	Yes	No
SELF-IMPOSED OBSTACLES		
I prefer performing operating tasks—not management functions—because I understand them better and I know how.	____	____
I can do the work in my unit better than anyone else.	____	____
I don't know how to delegate.	____	____
My employees won't like me if I expect too much of them.	____	____
I am not certain to whom I should delegate.	____	____
It is easier and quicker to do things myself.	____	____
We just can't afford to make any mistakes.	____	____
EMPLOYEE-IMPOSED OBSTACLES		
My employees lack experience and competence.	____	____
My employees are already overloaded.	____	____
My employees resist responsibility.	____	____
My employees fear criticism and avoid risk.	____	____

EXERCISE **(continued)**

	Yes	No
SITUATION-IMPOSED OBSTACLES		

Management expects me to handle the really important tasks personally. _____ _____

My employees can't be trusted to work on their own. _____ _____

We are seriously understaffed. I have no one to whom I can delegate. _____ _____

Most of our decisions are made under crisis conditions. _____ _____

If you answered yes to any of the above, you will find *Delegating for Results* most helpful.

Maddux, Robert. *Delegating for Results*, Menlo Park, CA: Crisp Publications, Inc. 1990. (The previous three exercises were reprinted with permission of the publisher.)

DELEGATION CHALLENGES FACING TECHNICAL SUPERVISORS

According to Earl Brooks, Professor of Administration at Cornell Graduate School of Business and Public Affairs, delegation is the process of establishing and maintaining effective working arrangements between a manager and the people who report to him or her. Delegation results when the performance of specified work is entrusted to another, and the results are mutually understood.

► **Determine with whom you can ''let go.''**

Are you currently doing more work than is necessary? (Because it is fun to do and you like to stay on top of your technology?) Or are there people available for you to delegate to? Perhaps it would be an opportunity for them to grow and develop and for you to learn new skills.

► **Select the appropriate strategy.**

Are you actually delegating or simply assigning a task? It is important to quickly learn to use each strategy. There is a critical communication and motivation difference and you need to know which one is most useful to use in each situation.

► **Be sensitive to the needs of others.**

How, what and why you delegate can be critical ''success determinants.'' Are you recognizing and addressing the unique expectations of your technical professionals? It is important to listen for both facts and feelings as you delegate to others.

► **Manage performance and monitor progress.**

A variety of technically sound systems exist to implement. Effective technical supervisors learn the techniques necessary to get ''extra-ordinary'' performance from ordinary people. Quality work is not an accident.''

While there are no magic formulas for successful delegation, we do know that those people who follow a plan are more successful than those who do not. Let's begin.

CHALLENGE #1: DETERMINE WITH WHOM YOU CAN "LET GO"

An Employee Skills and Interests Audit

As a technical supervisor, you continually have to assess what you *enjoy* doing versus what you *should* be doing. Since technology-driven organizations are often activity traps, it is very easy to be caught up in doing a lot of "things" eight to twelve hours a day, and yet not take care of your major job responsibilities. Again, "a lot may be going on, but little is taking place."

Let's assume you clearly know what your job responsibilities are. Are you now prepared to determine "who you can let go" to? This form may be valuable.

Exercise: Technical supervisors may want to complete this in a face-to-face meeting with the technical expert. A communication dialog will be initiated that should contribute both to the employee's motivation and to the supervisory delegation process.

Employee Name _____ Position _____

Particular area(s) of expertise: _____

The following statements are characteristics of work assignments. Please check all of the statements that indicate your general preferences for work projects. Your responses will help determine which projects are delegated to you.
I prefer projects that:

☐ Require team effort

☐ Are research oriented

☐ Require coordination with outside departments

☐ Require final briefings and presentations

☐ Allow me to work alone

☐ Are long-term rather than short-term projects

☐ Are outside my expertise

☐ Allow me to be completely in charge

CHALLENGE #2: SELECT THE APPROPRIATE STRATEGY

Technology-driven organizations generate enormous work loads. Not every activity is challenging for both technical supervisor and expert. In fact, some assignments might be dull, monotonous and unrewarding. The old adage, "No matter how you coat the pill, it's still a pill," is true.

But effective technical supervisors know how to identify and respond to the different requirements of task assignments and delegation no matter how dull the job. Each one has unique characteristics and requires specific steps for effectiveness.

Processes and Strategies

Part One: Am I Making Task Assignments Or Am I Delegating?

Characteristics of Task Assignments:

- Merely requires compliance.

- Is routine.

- Is demanded by the manager.

- Is known to the employee.

- The work originates in the employee's job description.

- Usually ongoing.

- Usually seen by employees as burdens.

- The appropriate leadership style is autocratic.

The main focus of a task assignment is action.

CHALLENGE #2 (continued)

Identify two examples of typical task assignments that you have recently made.

1. _____

2. _____

Characteristics of Delegation:

• Requires commitment.

• Produces growth.

• Must be negotiated.

• Could be misunderstood by the employee.

• Centers on a result or area of accountability.

• Usually has specific time parameters.

• Usually received as marks of respect or recognition for achievement.

• The appropriate leadership style is laissez-faire.

The main source of work is the manager's position description; it represents new ground to the employee.

Identify two examples of a typical delegation that you have recently made.

1. _____

2. _____

Time Out

If you know whether you are assigning tasks or delegating—and are prepared to use the right process to accomplish each—your communication, motivation and delegation skills will improve significantly.

Please take a moment to review this critically important step by responding to these statements:

I am currently assigning tasks. An example is: _____

_____

_____

I am currently delegating. An example is: _____

_____

_____

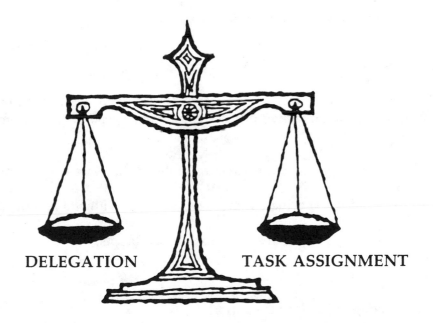

DELEGATION   TASK ASSIGNMENT

Adapted with permission from *Delegation: Getting It Right the First Time* by H. B. Karp. Personal Growth Systems. Copyright H. B. Karp.

Part Two: I Use the Following Specific Steps When I Make Task Assignments and When I Delegate.

Task Assignment Steps:

Not all work is challenging and fulfilling. Technical supervisors may have to make task assignments, that while necessary for meeting critical organizational needs, may not meet the needs of the individual. However, following these six steps may improve overall effectiveness:

1. Indicate what the additional task is and why it has to be done.

2. Briefly describe the specific details.

3. Ask for problems or reactions.

4. Honor employees' resistance.

5. Work with the situation.

6. Thank the employees for their forbearance.

Delegation Steps:

Delegation provides enormous opportunities to motivate and communicate with employees. This interactive process can be enhanced when you follow these six steps:

1. Inform the employee of the new responsibilities that you want to delegate.

2. Outline in detail the specific requirements that go with the responsibilities.

3. Ask for questions, suggestions, reactions or problems.

4. Negotiate.

5. Get a clear contract and offer support.

6. Thank the employee and express your confidence.

DELEGATION OR TASK ASSIGNMENT?

Now that you have gained an understanding of delegation and task assignment—and the appropriate steps to accomplish each—we would like to put your knowledge to the test.

Please read the following and determine:

1. Is it a situation requiring delegation, task assignment or both skills?

2. What appropriate steps would be most effective?

3. Outline a script that you would use to make the delegation and/or task assignment.

Situation A

You work for a large cooperative bank and supervise the work of eight credit analysts. A typical credit analyst has a degree in business or economics and two years of experience as a credit analyst.

You typically ask credit analysts for their assistance in the underwriting of commercial credit, which requires the ability to analyze corporate financial information for diversified industry groups. Your bank is experiencing healthy growth, and the work load and credit applications require continual prioritizing.

1. Does this situation require *delegation, task assignment* or *both skills*?

_____

2. What steps would you use?

- _____
  _____

- _____
  _____

- _____
  _____

CHALLENGE #2 (continued)

Situation B

As director of research and development for a world-renowned manufacturer of cosmetic and haircare products, you supervise the work of scientists. Scientists in your department typically have a B.S. in chemistry and a minimum of three to five years of experience in color cosmetics.

While your group provides backup for product development in a variety of hair lines, and may be involved in launching new products, your work is more tightly focused. Currently your chemists are working independently to provide technical evaluations for new raw materials and the renovation of existing product lines.

1. Does this situation require delegation, task assignment or both skills?

_____

2. What steps would you use?

● _____

_____

● _____

_____

● _____

_____

Situation C

You supervise the telecommunications department for a large university medical system. Ten data-entry operators work for you and support the functions of your department. A typical worker has a high school diploma and has completed a data-entry training course. Half your staff has one year previous experience in a health-care environment.

You are consistently monitoring their responsibility for keying information for the new data bases of the telephone, paging and voice-mail directories. They also perform data entry related to data circuits, cable infrastructure and on-call schedules for clinical and administrative staff.

1. Does this situation require *delegation, task assignment* or *both skills*?

_____

2. What steps would you use?

● _____

_____

● _____

_____

● _____

_____

Answers: Situation A is both delegation and task assignment. Situation B is currently task assignment. Situation C is permanently task assignment.

CHALLENGE #3: BE SENSITIVE TO THE NEEDS OF OTHERS

This workbook has continually focused on the unique characteristics of technical professionals and their technical supervisors. Here are additional suggestions for effective delegation to technical professionals.

Effective delegation to technical experts occurs when the technical supervisor:

- Realizes that technical experts are driven; they know their own strengths and needs

- Appreciates different styles and egos

- Relates short-term needs to long-range goals

- Generates a sense of accountability for both task and team

- Presents a challenge

- Keeps the process informal, yet structured

- Clearly defines requirements

- Shows application of employees' skills to delegated project

- Balances creative freedom with required constraints

- Provides a supportive environment balancing ''people'' and ''task''

- Clearly conveys accountability, yet maintains flexibility in the schedule for completion

- Balances coaxing and stifling

CHALLENGE #4: MANAGE PERFORMANCE AND MONITOR PROGRESS

One size does not fit all when it comes to monitoring the progress of your delegation or task assignment. Our earlier discussion introduced the concept of motivation and competence. We also talked about the importance of flexibility and style.

How you manage performance and monitor progress should take into consideration this simple model.

Performance = Motivation + Competence

In general, most of your subordinates will fall into one of four categories with respect to a particular assignment. The categories vary in terms of the employee's competence (ability to complete the assignment) and the employee's motivation (enthusiasm or willingness to complete the assignment).

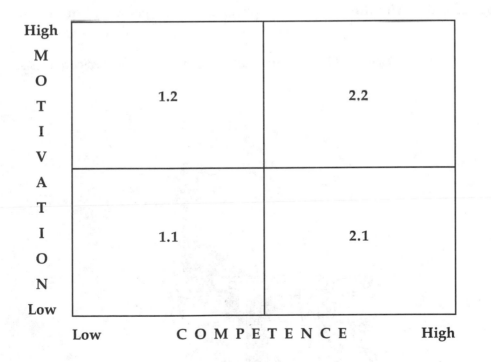

CHALLENGE #4 (continued)

Category Explanations

Employee Characteristics: 1.1 Low Competence/Low Motivation
Most Effective Monitoring: Provide frequent training and encouragement.

Employee Characteristics: 1.2 Low Competence/High Motivation
Most Effective Monitoring: Provide frequent training and occasional encouragement.

Employee Characteristics: 2.1 High Competence/Low Motivation
Most Effective Monitoring: Be available.

Employee Characteristics: 2.2 High Competence/High Motivation
Most Effective Monitoring: Provide positive encouragement, but plan to take corrective action.

3.0 Other: Does not fit into a neat category, but requires special analysis.

DELEGATION-STYLE FLEXIBILITY

Your effectiveness as a technical supervisor is directly related to your ability to make an assessment of an employee's supervisory needs, and to respond with appropriate monitoring style. This is especially true in delegating.

Four Cases

Exercise: Carefully review each of the following situations and then indicate the most effective monitoring style that you will use.

Employee A: Pat, Integration Design Engineer

Pat is an integration design engineer with seven years of experience in designing microprocessor-based military systems. Pat is well liked and active in a variety of community and professional organizations. While your organization has introduced a flexible career-path program, Pat has indicated little interest in moving ahead and would like to remain in the mid-level technical professional track.

What monitoring style would you use for Pat? _____

Employee B: Karol, Field Technician

Karol is a field technician with experience in construction, heavy equipment and groundwater testing for environmental-remediation projects. Karol applied for the position of field supervisor that you now hold. The job required demonstrated ability to manage several projects simultaneously that you—as the off-the street candidate—possessed, but Karol did not. Since being passed up for the position, Karol's work has deteriorated.

What monitoring style would you use for Karol? _____

CHALLENGE #4 (continued)

Employee C: Lee, Photo Therapy Technician

Lee is a photo therapy technician in a large, rapidly growing multispecialty group medical practice. Lee treats patients with established photo therapy protocols quite effectively. However, in front-office work, especially in maintaining records, there is not even minimal acceptable performance. Additional training and coaching by a co-worker has not produced any improvement.

What monitoring style would you use for Lee? _____

Employee D: Jordan, Technical Integration Specialist and Sales

Jordan has strong knowledge of computer hardware and software, as well as extensive bar-coding experience with a large federal agency. Now part of a sales team of technical integration specialists (in data collection for manufacturing, distribution and health care), Jordan is having difficulty.

More specifically, Jordan took this position because it appeared to be an excellent opportunity not only to use proven technical skills, but also to make more money. While sales prospects have been developed relatively well, there has been trouble closing contracts and meeting monthly sales quotas.

What monitoring style would you use for Jordan? _____

Answers: With Pat use monitoring style 2.2; Karol: 2.1; Lee: 1.2; Jordan: 3.0. Jordan is both motivated and competent. The deficiency is in a specific area—"closing the sale,"—which needs to be addressed by special training focused in that one area.

THREE DELEGATION RECOMMENDATIONS

1. Delegate Those Things That You Know Best.

While this recommendation may first sound silly, it actually makes sense the more you think about it. In fact, the people who study the characteristics of successful technical supervisors make several observations that support this statement. First, the technical supervisors who delegate what they know best can more effectively monitor the performance of the staff member. They quickly know what is being done correctly and what needs improvement.

Second, one way to move ahead is to train someone to do your job. By delegating you *share,* instead of *hoard,* knowledge. And in our new learning society, this gives *you* a chance to learn new things.

2. Approach Delegation As a Risk-Taking Behavior.

There can be no doubt that each time you decide to delegate a specific task to a specific individual, you are taking a risk. Many times technical supervisors may find their organization encouraging frequency and depth in delegation on one hand, then taking harsh, punitive measures when the results are not perfect.

You are in the best position to determine when, where and how to delegate. There will always be situational trade-offs between delegating an assignment to a less, experienced employee who may profit from mastering a new task, but take more time to do it, or giving it to that "proven pro" who can get it done quickly and effectively. Risks of quality, time and cost will all influence your choice. There are no magic answers.

3. Identify the Level of Technical Knowledge Loss You Are Willing to Experience.

You will have to make a choice at one or more points in your career about how much loss in technical knowledge you are willing to experience. A technical career path allows the expert to grow and develop as a technical leader. The management career path emphasizes management in and of technology. The better you become at managing technical experts and projects, fully using the best delegation skills, the more depth and breath of technical knowledge you will give up. Your decision should be free, complete and without remorse.

TECHNICAL SUPERVISORS' DELEGATION LESSONS

Previous workbook sections gave you the chance to meet these experienced technical supervisors. So far they have offered recommendations for making the transition from technical expert to supervisor, and developing communication and motivation skills.

They are back again to answer two questions about delegation skills for technical supervisors. After you review their advice, answer two questions that relate their experiences to yours.

Technical Supervisor #1: Taylor, Group Leader

---

1. *What specific challenges did you experience in delegating to technical professionals?*

   Delegating to someone over whom I don't have direct control (like using a centralized technical support center, or even my boss). Talk about living with fear and uncertainty!

2. *What specific recommendations would you make to help other technical professionals develop their delegation skills?*

   Get to know your staff so you can learn to trust (or not) their abilities. Monitor what they are doing *during* the effort rather than at the end, so you can work together to make adjustments. Don't be the person who has only negative comments when their effort is completed.

Technical Supervisor #2: Caton, Director, Program Development

---

1. *What specific challenges did you experience in delegating to technical professionals?*
   Overcoming the feeling that I am expected to do it all, or that since I am now accountable, I must do it all to make certain it is done correctly.

2. *What specific recommendations would you make to help other technical professionals develop their delegation skills?*

   Resist the "need" to do everything yourself. Don't think your staff expects you to know it all. Accept the risk that someone may not do the task as well as, or like, you would, but that they will do well enough, and they will get better with experience.

Technical Supervisor #3: Pat, Principal Investigator

---

1. *What specific challenges did you experience in delegating to technical professionals?*

I quickly saw that it took others longer to do what I did, and the results were inferior. It was tempting to, and I confess I did, snatch work back and do it myself.

2. *What specific recommendations would you make to help other technical professionals develop their delegation skills?*

Document tasks you are delegating, and give due dates. Put everything in writing. Keep a log of the date, time and place of work delegated. What worked? Didn't work? You will need this record in case you have to take corrective action.

Technical Supervisor #4: Shawn, Chief, Space Intelligence

---

1. *What specific challenges did you experience in delegating to technical professionals?*

In some cases people do not wish to be in charge of anything, so have remained where they feel comfortable and happy in their work. But even though I have heard, ''I don't want to supervise,'' from several people, they will gladly volunteer to take charge of training for new hires, or other side-tasks, and slowly they find that they can supervise and still enjoy their work.

2. *What specific recommendations would you make to help other technical professionals develop their delegation skills?*

The only way that I got where I am today is that my boss, who held the job for 24 years, placed a variety of responsibilities upon me, and these tasks gave me the experience I needed to do my job today. I do the same with my current employees, and as I stated earlier, once a task is given, a technical professional will become very creative.

TECHNICAL SUPERVISORS' DELEGATION LESSONS (continued)

Lessons Learned

1. What are the similarities between the experiences you have had delegating and those of our supervisors?

_____

_____

_____

_____

_____

_____

2. Did any of their recommendations have special value?

_____

_____

_____

_____

_____

_____

_____

P A R T

V

Planning for Further Development

DEVELOP A PLAN OF ACTION

You can now harness "lessons learned" and plan your next steps. The exercises, readings and assessments in this book provided you with a better understanding of the knowledge, skills and attitudes that you may already possess, as well as those you need to develop. The following exercise serves as a vehicle to develop a plan of action.

Part I: Affirming Your Current Strengths

My current supervisory skills are (list the three strongest):

1. _____

2. _____

3. _____

I have evidence of my success in each of these areas. Examples are:

1. _____

2. _____

3. _____

Part II: Developing Additional Skills

Complete the matrix on the following page, which parallels the content of the workbook. Suggestions: There are many ways to develop as a technical supervisor beyond reading a book and taking a seminar or course. Consider the following options when completing "How I will develop." Many are perfect motivational matches for technical superviosrs.

- Learn from others who will coach and counsel (experts and mentors)

- Participate in professional associations, conferences and conventions

- Rotate jobs, seek enrichment or a lateral transfer

- Take on special, time-limited assignments: by myself, with other team members or with other operating units in our organization.

- Find opportunities to train others, lead projects or meetings, and make presentations

Skill Development Matrix

What other nontraditional developmental activities exist for you?

DEVELOPMENTAL NEED	WHEN I WILL INITIATE DEVELOPMENT	HOW IT WILL BE DEVELOPED
Transitioning		
Communicating		
Motivating		
Delegating		
Other		

Additional People Resources Matrix

The following individuals could assist me in my development.

RESOURCE	HOW CAN THEY ASSIST?
Supervisor	
Peers	
Staff	
Other	

MANAGE YOUR JOB AND ADVANCE YOUR CAREER

Technical experts who transition into technical supervision are often academic and technical purists. Loyalty to their discipline and technology as well as their high level of ethical standards can sometimes impede their job effectiveness and career advancement.

Here are specific recommendations for technical supervisors who achieve success.

Manage Your Job

Hard work and high ideals do not always ensure success. You manage your job effectively when you:

- Take a job only when it matches your present and potential strengths and it pleases you.

- Don't hoard or monopolize your job too long. Learn yours quickly, document success and then move onto another more challenging opportunity.

- Make sure that your boss is pleased with your performance.

- Recognize that leadership is waiting to be assumed. Don't spend time arguing for neat, formal job descriptions. They will only trap you.

Advance Your Career

Ultimately, you are responsible for advancing your career. It is always great to have a manager who takes a personal and professional interest in you. A clear organizational career path is also of assistance. But, *you* will have to take care of you.

- **Prioritize time to manage your career.** Simply doing your job well does not assure success—become your own public relations agent.

- **Make sure that you are noticed.** Your career will be significantly enhanced when senior managers are consistently observing your achievements.

- **Volunteer and nominate yourself.** Step forward and suggest ''I can do it.'' Don't wait for someone to discover how great you really are.

- **Get off the field when you don't like the game.** Too many technical experts have been railroaded, by themselves (for salary increases) or management (by necessity), into the role of supervisor. You may want to seek other career options when this describes you.

POLITICS CAN BE FUN

For many trained technical experts, there is only one kind of "power"—technical expertise. And for these people, organizational politics is a waste of time. But technical supervisors who survive and thrive in technology-driven organizations are successful at politics. Here are some recommendations:

1. Organizational politics are unavoidable.

Getting what you need, and giving others what they need, requires skill at politics, negotiation and influence.

2. Don't underestimate the effective behavior of management or the organization.

Avoid association with those who suffer from acute melancholia and conduct formal organizational cynic clinics. Model and support positive behavior.

3. Build your political network.

Develop senior management champions, or referent power, who can keep an eye out for you and help you manage your job and advance your career.

4. Keep your integrity.

Your increasingly higher technical supervisory positions will cause you to have contact with increasingly higher organizational stakeholders. Questions of "ethics," "fairness" and "legality" may come up. Your integrity as an individual is critical to your success.

TECHNICAL SUPERVISORS' FINAL RECOMMENDATIONS

Each of the experienced technical supervisors whom we have previously met has offered guidance. This is the last time we will hear from them. Once again, respond to their advice by answering two questions that relate that their experiences to yours.

Technical Supervisor #1: Taylor, Group Leader

What specific recommendations would you make to a technical expert who is now planning and managing a career as a technical supervisor or manager?

Keep up your technical skills (as much as you can) and keep learning new things. Learn about your external *and* internal clients. Maintain your contacts. Take advantage of opportunities to work with other departments, so they get to know you. Always look for ways to improve your management skills. Be receptive to change. Learn to manage your time and priorities.

Technical Supervisor #2: Caton, Director, Program Development

What specific recommendations would you make to a technical expert who is now planning and managing a career as a technical supervisor or manager?

Keep abreast of technical developments. Network inside and outside of the company (with sincerity). Work hard; be willing to commit. Get an MBA.

Technical Supervisor #3: Pat, Principal Investigator

What specific recommendations would you make to a technical expert who is now planning and managing a career as a technical supervisor or manager?

Document your training and development activities. Plan ahead for future opportunities.

TECHNICAL SUPERVISORS' FINAL RECOMMENDATIONS (continued)

> **Technical Supervisor #4:** Shawn, Chief, Space Intelligence

What specific recommendations would you make to a technical expert who is now planning and managing a career as a technical supervisor or manager?

The people who work for you have to think of their own positions. You must pay special attention to getting them the classes they require to move forward and to increase their pay and benefits. I have one worker who is maxed out in terms of salary steps, yet is very happy in his work. I can occasionally give him a small cash award, or my parking pass for a week.

Lessons Learned

1. What are the similarities between your experiences and those of our supervisors?

_____

_____

_____

_____

_____

2. Did any of their recommendations have special value for you?

_____

_____

_____

_____

_____

Congratulations On Your Career Move.
Good Luck!

P A R T

Appendix

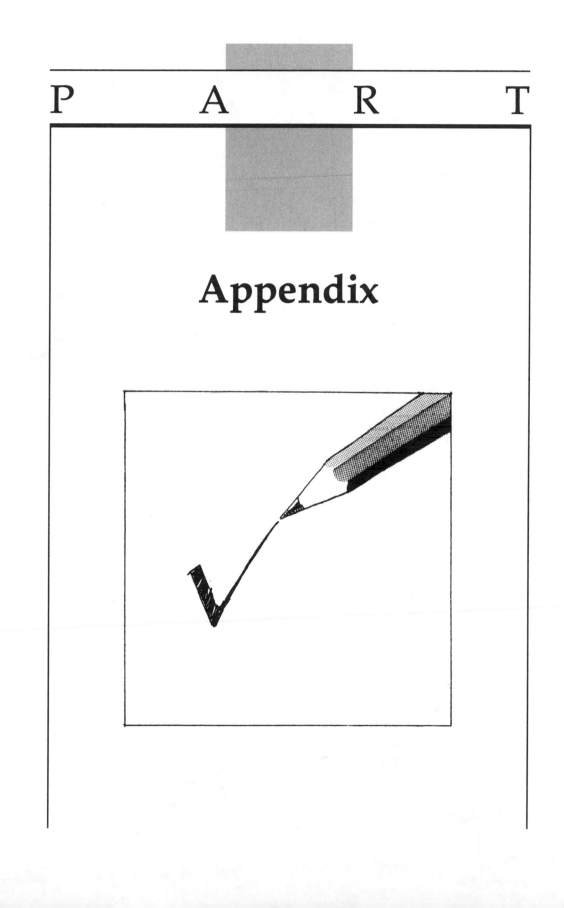

BIBLIOGRAPHY

The following books may also be of special interest to you. They each address, as this book has done, what is unique about technical people, projects and environments.

Badawy, M. K. *Developing Managerial Skills in Engineers and Scientists.* New York: Van Nostrand Reinhold Company, 1982.

Broadwell, Martin B., and Ruth Sizemore House. *Supervising Technical and Professional People.* New York: John Wiley & Sons, 1986.

Gray, James G. Jr. *Strategies and Skills of Technical Presentations: A Guide for Professionals in Business and Industry.* New York: Quorum Books, 1988.

House, Ruth Sizemore. *The Human Side of Project Management.* Reading, Massachusetts: Addison-Wesley Publishing Company, 1988.

Jackson, Dale E. *Interpersonal Communication for Technically-Trained Managers: A Guide to Skills and Techniques.* New York: Quorum Books, 1988.

Karp, H. B. *Delegation: Getting It Right the First Time.* Personal Growth Systems.

Kirkpatrick, Donald L. "Management Development," *Human Resources and Management Handbook.* Edited by William R. Tracey, New York: American Management Association. 1985. p 931.

Kleingartner, Archie, and Carolyn S. Anderson. *Human Resource Management in High Technology Firms.* Lexington, Mass.: Lexington Books, 1987.

Maddux, Robert. *Delegating for Results.* Menlo Park, Calif.: Crisp Publications, Inc., 1990.

Miller, Donald Britton. *Managing Professionals in Research and Development: A Guide for Improving Productivity and Organization Effectiveness.* San Francisco: Jossey-Bass Publishers, 1990. ISBN 1-55542-000-1

Silverman, Melvin. *The Technical Manager's Survival Book.* New York: McGraw-Hill Book Company, 1984.

Von Glinow, Mary Ann. *The New Professionals: Managing Today's High-Tech Employees.* Cambridge, Mass.: Harper & Row Publishers, Inc., 1988.

Weinberg, Gerald M. *Becoming a Technical Leader: An Organic Problem-Solving Approach.* New York: Dorset House Publishing, 1989.

TECHNICAL SUPERVISOR QUESTIONNAIRE

**Making the Transition from Expert to Manager
Case Study Questionnaire**

Name_____ Title_____

Organization_____ Phone_____

Address_____ City/State/ZIP_____

Thank you for assisting in the research efforts for *From Technical Specialist to Supervisor*. The information you supply will be used to increase the relevance of material appearing in future editions of this book.

Please answer the following questions as completely as you can. Your material will be treated confidentially.

1. Educational Background and Degrees:

2. Technical Specialty and Experience:

3. Why did you take your first technical supervisor position?

4. Did you have any difficulty in making the transition from a technical specialist to supervising the work of other technical professionals?

5. What specific challenges did you experience, as a new technical supervisor, in each of these areas?

- Communicating with technical professionals:

- Motivating technical professionals:

- Delegating to technical professionals:

6. How long have you been a supervisor or manager?

7. What are your current and future career goals?

8. What specific recommendations, building on your rich experience, would you make to a technical expert making that first transition to technical supervision, in these five areas?

    a. Making an effective transition:

    b. Developing communication skills for technical professionals:

    c. Developing an understanding of how to motivate technical professionals:

    d. Developing delegation skills:

    e. Planning and managing a career as a technical supervisor or manager:

Thank you for taking the time to complete this questionnaire. In appreciation for your efforts, you will receive a complimentary copy of the newsletter, *Focus on HRD* (Human Resource Development) published biannually by OD&R. Please fax or send your survey to:

Dr. Donald Shandler
Organizational Development and Research Associates, Inc. (OD&R™)
Technical Supervision Institute
10480 Little Patuxent Parkway, Suite 400
Columbia, Maryland 21044
Phone: 410/750-2400 Fax: 410/750-3937

NOTES

NOTES

NOTES

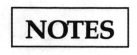

NOTES

NOTES

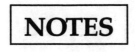

NOTES

NOTES

NOTES